THANKS
FOR THE
MEMORIES,
GEORGE

D1025362

Also by Mike Loew

Tough Call
Citizen You!

THANKS
FOR THE
MEMORIES,
GEORGE

WHAT EIGHT YEARS OF BUSH WILL
DO TO A COUNTRY

MIKE LOEW

THREE RIVERS PRESS • NEW YORK

Copyright © 2009 by Mike Loew

Published in the United States by Three Rivers Press, an imprint of the
Crown Publishing Group, a division of Random House, Inc., New York.
www.crownpublishing.com

Three Rivers Press and the Tugboat design are registered trademarks
of Random House, Inc.

Library of Congress Cataloging-in-Publication data is available
upon request.

ISBN 978-0-307-46286-2

Printed in the United States of America

Design by Maria Elias
Charts designed by Brandon Kizart-Haynes
Photograph in frontmatter: Getty Images

10 9 8 7 6 5 4 3 2 1

First Edition

for George

CONTENTS

THANKS
FOR THE
MEMORIES,
GEORGE

Introduction

WHERE TO BEGIN?

The time has come to say good-bye to our fearless leader, George W. Bush. Here he comes now. How are you, George? This is such an honor to watch you leave office. You're looking good, Mr. President. Haggard and senile, but good. Yes sir, good old Dubya. You always were quick to hand out the nicknames, but we've got a few for you, too: Flubya. Incurious George. Spurious George. Shrub. *El Arbusto Pequeño*. The Decider. The Commander Guy. Financial Asset of Khalid Bin Mahfouz. The Texecutioner. Head Cheerleader. Torturer-in-Chief. The Kinda Guy We'd Wanna Have a Beer With. Daddy's Little War Criminal. Disaster Monkey. The Illegal Occupant. That Fucking Asshole Bush. The Bogus POTUS. Walker, Texas Danger. DUI Case Number 2342, 09/04/76, Kennebunkport, Maine. We know him by so many names, but the time has come for George W. Bush to pass on the torch of liberty, which he hath dampened with his own pizzle for eight long years. Actually, just give us the torch now, George, we'll take it back to camp while you stay out here alone in this filthy swamp of failure that you've gotten us into.

George W. Bush had America by the nuts for eight years. For those Americans without nuts, allow me to explain what this feels like. The nuts are the source of vim and vigor, providing drive and motivation throughout the entire body and mind. This nut-generated energy can be used for sexual purposes, of course, to help create the miracle of new life, but can also be applied to work, sport, art, music, finally organizing that unruly sock drawer, and a host of other worthwhile pursuits. These precious twin orbs provide the will to live, but are also extremely tender and sensitive. The clammy hand of George W. Bush clenched around the nuts of America over these eight miserable years first began with excruciating pain, which turned to outrage and panic, and finally led to a numb, dazed, zombielike existence that seemed as if it would never end. George W. Bush squeezed the very life out of America's nuts. I can't even imagine what effect he had on our ovaries.

Bush has been the most uncaring, deceitful, arrogant, proudly ignorant, and moronically belligerent president in the history of our republic. He managed to embody the viciousness of Richard Nixon, the stupidity of Gerald Ford, the falseness of Ronald Reagan, and the warmongering of Genghis Khan, all disguised by appearing to be as dumb as a slice of Texas toast. But perhaps we shouldn't be so hard on Bush. After all, he suffers from a rare form of sociopathic speech disorder. This means that whatever Bush says, he in fact means the reverse of it. For example, when Bush says "peace," he actually means "war." When he says "freedom," he means "extended tours of duty." When he says "patriotic," he means "treasonous." If you knew about Bush's speech disorder and were able to translate his words with his condition in mind, your blood pressure probably stayed a little more stable over the last eight years—a good thing given the cost of health insurance nowadays.

As these words are written, in the fading light from the dying embers of the Bush presidency, there is one burning question that leaps to mind, addressed to the next generation of Americans: Is the country still standing? Kind of? Or are armed personnel carriers rolling through the streets, with Darth Vader–styled riot cops guarding the supermarkets, staring down shuffling queues of rapidly thinning consumers as they wait for their weekly rations of Doritos Collisions Hot-Wings-and-Blue-Cheese–Flavored Tortilla Chips™? That is the overwhelming emotional state of angst and paranoia that living under the shadow of Bush has given us—that the sky could really, truly fall at any time. Not since the days of Herbert Hoover have Americans so obsessively checked their cupboards to see how many canned goods they have, just in case. Bush always seized upon the disasters that befell us through his neglect, such as 9/11, the aftermath of Hurricane Katrina, and the financial crisis of 2008, to advance his agenda. If anyone raised his voice to say something like "Maybe invading Iraq is a bad idea," Bush unleashed a storm of panic and fear, telling us that no one was safe unless we followed along exactly with what he wanted. Bush's favorite line in a movie is from the killer police robot ED-209 in *RoboCop,* "You have thirty seconds to comply."

What was the real end goal of the Bush administration? Due to its actions, it's a world where national governments and international law have no meaning; where unjustified military

President Bush's Greatest Moments—The Near Future

Paul J. Richards/AFP/Getty Images

Our retired unitary-executive appointee enjoys
his new freedom at a private resort.

The Road Warrior/Warner Bros.

George W. Bush's future vision for America.

invasions (including private military corporations as mercenary troops) are unleashed to steal resources; where democracy is suppressed and human rights are violated through torture, surveillance, and secret police pressure; and where common people have no defense against corporate polluters, occupying armies, or secretive financial manipulation. We got screwed repeatedly by Bush, and now we've all got a nasty STD.

He maintained an endlessly surprising run, all the way to the end. Even now, with only a few weeks left to go, we wonder if George still has one more trick up his sleeve. "There's no way they can sneak in an attack on Iran before they leave office, right? Not with the way the economy has crashed. That's like a one-in-a-million Hail Mary shot, but you never know with these guys ..." We've all wondered if Bush would "miraculously" capture or kill Osama bin Laden at the end of his term. Or better yet, if he dedicated his retirement to hunting Osama through the highlands of Waziristan, and finally bagged the terrorist mastermind with a long-range sniper rifle, would anyone even care?

There is a general sense of growing intangibility in our lives. Solid things that you could once count on, like rules and contracts and jobs and paychecks, have all evaporated. You used to have to work if you wanted to get paid, but in Bush's America, Dick Cheney's Halliburton cronies can dump a truckload of gravel on the ground in Iraq and call it a school, while they pocket billions of U.S. taxpayer money with a sweet no-bid government contract. Every time we voted during the Bush years, millions of ballots that were picked up, read, and rocked with the vote of a real-live American were tossed into the trash for technical imperfections, especially in black neighborhoods. Globalist free-trade agreements were promised to make life

Bush's Approval Ratings

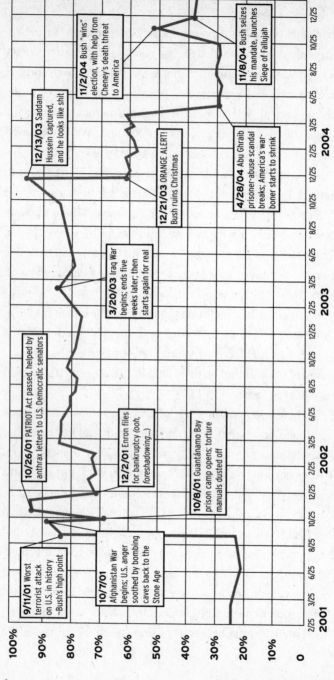

9/11/01 Worst terrorist attack on U.S. in history —Bush's high point

10/7/01 Afghanistan War begins; U.S. anger soothed by bombing caves back to the Stone Age

10/8/01 Guantánamo Bay prison camp opens; torture manuals dusted off

10/26/01 PATRIOT Act passed, helped by anthrax letters to U.S. Democratic senators

12/2/01 Enron files for bankruptcy (ooh, foreshadowing...)

3/20/03 Iraq War begins; ends five weeks later; then starts again for real

12/13/03 Saddam Hussein captured, and he looks like shit

12/21/03 ORANGE ALERT! Bush ruins Christmas

11/2/04 Bush "wins" election, with help from Cheney's death threat to America

4/28/04 Abu Ghraib prisoner-abuse scandal breaks; America's war-boner starts to shrink

11/8/04 Bush seizes his mandate, launches Siege of Fallujah

6

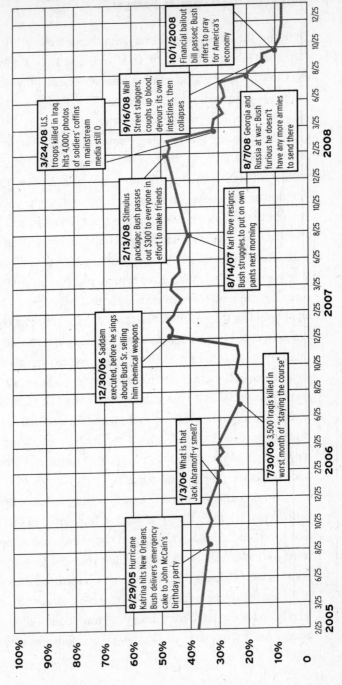

8/29/05 Hurricane Katrina hits New Orleans, Bush delivers emergency cake to John McCain's birthday party

1/3/06 What is that Jack Abramoff-y smell?

7/30/06 3,500 Iraqis killed in worst month of "staying the course"

12/30/06 Saddam executed, before he sings about Bush Sr. selling him chemical weapons

8/14/07 Karl Rove resigns; Bush struggles to put on own pants next morning

2/13/08 Stimulus package; Bush passes out $300 to everyone in effort to make friends

3/24/08 U.S. troops killed in Iraq hits 4,000; photos of soldiers' coffins in mainstream media still 0

8/7/08 Georgia and Russia at war; Bush furious he doesn't have any more armies to send there

9/16/08 Wall Street staggers, coughs up blood, devours its own intestines, then collapses

10/1/2008 Financial bailout bill passed; Bush offers to pray for America's economy

100% 90% 80% 70% 60% 50% 40% 30% 20% 10% 0

2/25 3/25 6/25 8/25 10/25 12/25 2/25 3/25 6/25 8/25 10/25 12/25 2/25 3/25 6/25 8/25 10/25 12/25 2/25 3/25 6/25 8/25 10/25 12/25

2005   2006   2007   2008

7

better for the American workers, who then watched their factories and jobs get shipped off to Mexico and Malaysia. While the CEOs of these manufacturing companies earn hundreds of millions a year, their former employees hold garage sales in an effort to make their mortgage payments.

Without any goods being manufactured in the United States, our leading industry has become finance—the manipulation and gambling of other people's money. Credit derivatives are endlessly swapped back and forth, until we are told that it's all worthless and that our life savings that we spent the best years of our lives to build are now slashed in half. (Hopefully that last phrase won't be too painfully dated a few weeks from now.) Everywhere you looked in Bush's America, there was the growing sense that we were just being written out of the equation here. We didn't matter anymore. We didn't count, especially on Election Day in 2000 when the majority of us voted for Al Gore. If you weren't in the secret strike force of George W. Bush's military/intelligence/governmental/financial elite, the message over the last eight years is that you might as well just shut up and fuck off. The joyous celebration over Barack Obama's victory was the sound of a nation of ghosts gleefully reassuming their warm, red-blooded bodies again, if only for one night.

Think of this volume as a heartwarming scrapbook of the Bush years. It's been a very important time in all of our lives that we should cherish. You can fold your newspaper clippings from 9/11 into this book, or appliqué your old keys to your home in New Orleans that still hasn't been repaired. This book is the perfect place to display a photograph of your husband who hasn't come back from Iraq yet. How about a decorative border made from your 401(k) statements, showing a steadily dropping balance? A receipt from a gas station when it cost half as much to fill up your tank can make for an attractive bookmark. Don't forget to include a bit of duct tape and plastic wrap from your home protection kit against anthrax. Memories really are important.

This book collects all the low points, as well as the abysmal points, of the last eight years. We must take the time to reflect upon the treaties that have been broken, the invasions that have been launched, the people who have been tortured, the globe that has been warmed, and the elections that have been stolen. Let us sail back through the memories, floating on the slapping waves of corruption that Bush left in his oily wake. It's a salty, sloppy ride, but take heart. It is crucially important that we remember George W. Bush very clearly. The more you look at Bush's record, the more you realize how much we've lost. And Bush tried so hard to make us forget what it was that we had lost in the first place. The Iraq War is still a rotting albatross around our neck, but Bush's "surge" was touted as a way to make us not mind the smell so much. It's hard to think back to a time before this stinking corpse was thrown over our shoulders, we've all grown so used to it. But when you remember that distant moment in the past, you realize what Bush has taken from you, and you get angry. You want to bring back the good old days, when this nation wasn't at war, torturing prisoners, spying on Americans, and bombing the shit out of poor villages with unmanned Predator drones. Never let them convince us again that the best way to stop foreign terrorists who hate America is by unleashing bloodshed and panic across the globe.

As outlined in their 1997 policy paper, *The Project for the New American Century,* Bush and his neoconservative elite plotted nothing less than total domination of the planet Earth. They advocated the unlimited use of U.S. military power anywhere in the world, in order to dominate natural resources and prevent the rise of any nation that could rival them. They even wrote of the usefulness of researching biological weapons that could target specific racial genotypes of humans. But they acknowledged that the American people might be reluctant to take on this role of world-killers. They stated that "the process of transformation, even if it brings revolutionary change, is likely to be a long one, absent some catastrophic and catalyzing event, like a new Pearl Harbor." As soon as they got their Pearl Harbor on September 11, 2001, the Bush administration crashed onto the world stage with a shocking application of military force—then slowly staggered and crumbled once those conflicts didn't end, but kept going and going and going.

George W. Bush has one arrest for driving while under the influence of alcohol. Not to be outdone, Dick Cheney has two drunk-driving busts on his permanent record. Both Bush and Cheney brought solid, real-world experience to the White House of getting wasted, hopping behind the wheel of a car, and roaring off down the road. This is as perfect a metaphor as any to describe the nightmare of the Bush years—he and Cheney are drunk off their asses driving the SUV, while you're trapped in the backseat, eyeballs bulging in terror as you rocket down the road. Incredibly painful-looking problems loom in front of you on the highway, which Bush ricochets off of. The glancing collisions tear off chunks of your vehicle; you hear terrible grinding noises and smell burning rubber. You can't move, with ten seat belts strapping you down. Through the front windshield, you see the road is about to end, right in

Looking Back

In his own view, what are George W. Bush's best and worst memories from his White House years?

Memory	Best	Worst
Katrina	Giving billions to Halliburton and Bechtel to rebuild New Orleans; Dick Cheney and George Schultz lick his feet with gratitude	Flying to New Orleans for all of those sweaty photo ops where he had to hug hurricane survivors
War	Watching the glorious looting of Baghdad in March 2003	Laura demanding that he get rid of the 900-pound stone head of Ba'al that he worships in his den
Sex	Greeting King Abdullah of Saudi Arabia with a tender kiss on the lips	Caught masturbating to Abu Ghraib torture porn video by Lynne Cheney
Drugs	Confiscating daughter Jenna's weed stash and giving her a lecture on the dangers of drugs; she learns and grows from this experience	Snapping awake three weeks later, on the deck of an aircraft carrier, wearing a flight suit
Campaign	Getting the congratulation call from John Kerry in 2004 on his secret Skull and Bones hotline	Being told he couldn't run in 2008
Fitness	Strenuous workouts with Jeff Gannon that didn't leave marks—only impressions	Having to cut back on workout schedule, as Iraq was blowing up
Iraq	Thinking up the name Operation Iraqi Liberation all by himself, chuckling at the clever acronym	Being told by Ari Fleischer that he had to change it to Operation Iraqi Freedom a few days later
9/11	Seeing the first plane hit the World Trade Center on TV, before it was televised nationally	Accidentally saying that on national TV
al-Qaeda	Getting that Osama bin Laden tape out just four days before the election in 2004	Receiving the sad news from his Saudi Arabian friends that Osama bin Laden had passed on

front of a bottomless chasm. Bush hits the gas. The SUV soars off the cliff. George and Dick look at each other with a devilish grin, simultaneously yelling "Bailout!" Bush slams a button on the dashboard, and he and Cheney pop out of the top of the car in ejector seats. Golden parachutes open above them as they float away, cackling.

Bill Clinton was roundly accused of being a bad influence on the moral fiber of the nation. His sexual shenanigans may have contributed to an increase in oral sex among teenagers, which was a source of distress to all segments of society (except teenaged boys). But is George W. Bush to blame for an even more corruptive attack on the morals of America? Bush is a rule bender, a lawbreaker, a guy who does a terrible job but touts phony symbols of achievement while he's off on the side working toward his own selfish goals. Bush always cheated the system, ignoring the old-fashioned expectations that you try to do a good job, you pull for your team, and then get paid fairly for your work. Bush is opposed to the idea of America as a meritocracy and has lashed out against it repeatedly, always preferring to enrich his well-connected cronies instead of doing anything to better the nation.

You see this kind of Bush-inspired behavior everywhere now in this country: stockbrokers selling phony wealth; school systems inflating grades to pass federally required test scores; our government going into trillions of dollars of debt to China with no collateral; our military exaggerating terrorist KIA lists (how many second lieutenants does Osama bin Laden have?); even our athletes juicing up on steroids to unfairly dominate on the field. This is the Win at Any Cost mentality (WAAC, pronounced "wack"), where the severe risks of crashing the financial system, killing thousands of civilians, or shrinking

A Pattern Emerges

How did President Bush treat whistleblowers who revealed tragic blunders and corruption, and how did he reward criminal traitors who made him feel better about himself in comparison?

Name and Position	Job Performance	Treatment
Sibel Edmonds, FBI translator, 2001–2002	Revealed that U.S. nuclear secrets were stolen and sold on the black market with the help and protection of high-ranking U.S. officials	Fired by the FBI and placed under a federal gag order that forbids her to testify in court or reveal the names of the people involved
Gen. Richard Myers, acting head of the U.S. military's Joint Chiefs of Staff on 9/11/01	Sat in a meeting on Capitol Hill while both World Trade Towers and then the Pentagon were struck by airliners	Promoted to chairman of the Joint Chiefs of Staff on October 1, 2001
Coleen Rowley, FBI agent, 1980–2004	Wrote a letter to FBI Director Robert Mueller on how FBI HQ had ignored and quashed warnings about the 9/11 attacks	Rowley's criticisms used by the FBI to roll back rules against indiscriminate domestic spying on U.S. citizens
Gen. Ralph Eberhart, chief of North American Aerospace Defense Command (NORAD) on 9/11/01	Inexplicably failed to order an effective air defense of the U.S. during the 9/11 attacks	Promoted to head the new "Northern Command" established in 2002
Dan Rather, anchorman of CBS Evening News from 1981–2005	Drew attention to Bush's shameful National Guard record during the Vietnam War	Rather's documents were falsely claimed to be forgeries; he "retired" four months later; now works at a falafel cart
Gen. Eric Shinseki, Chief of Staff of the U.S. Army, 1999–2003	Cautioned before invasion that several hundred thousand troops would be needed to stabilize postwar Iraq	Ignored and ridiculed by former Secretary of Defense and Bush appointee Donald Rumsfeld
Paul Wolfowitz, Deputy Secretary of Defense, 2001–2005	Claimed that Iraqis would greet U.S. troops as liberators, and that Iraqi oil revenues would pay for the war	Promoted to be president of the World Bank in 2005, a position he held for two years until he fucked that one up, too

your own testicles into dry little raisins are ignored. The only thing that matters to the WAAC is grabbing as much money and power as they can, which they will have all to themselves. Then they get to sit alone in the deepest chamber of their secret Skull and Bones fraternity, smirking at all the barbarians out there while they stroke the skull of Geronimo, which their grandfather stole, and admire the size of their bank account balance. Good times.

We've all been dragging our feet for years now, over-whelmed by Bush fatigue. But now that he's finally gone, we have to take a hard look at the wreckage that we're in. It's like those moments in your life when you lose your way for a while. Maybe you got divorced, or maybe you lost your job, and the empty pizza boxes have really piled up, when suddenly you have that moment when you realize, Hey, I don't *have* to be miserable anymore. And Christ, I really have to clean up all this shit that's lying around my house. It's time to dig down into that clogged garbage disposal, time to clear out Bush's slimy hair balls from the shower drain of America.

Born into extreme wealth and privilege, Bush is all about making messes and waltzing off. Someone else has to clean up after him, just like they always have. It feels like our entire nation has been transformed into little George's personal staff of maids. That would make Barack Obama the maid-in-chief, and he's already calling for a period of mandatory national service for American youths to clean up after Bush's dirty dia-pers. Bush is just like whoever spilled a pint of half-and-half all over the condiments cart at the coffee shop and didn't wipe it up, even though there's a whole box full of goddamn nap-kins *right there*. Of course, Bush doesn't just spill milk on a counter, he's more on the level of spilling radioactive uranium into our rivers or trashing the entire economy.

No matter how bad it got, Bush always looked like he was having a great time. He came across like a carefree, smirking chimpanzee, although his hairy finger was the one on the nuclear-war button. His shoulders would bob up and down when he cackled with glee, like a badly animated cartoon villain (Skeletor comes to mind). It was all cute nicknames and slaps on the back, while people were actually dying because of him. Yeah, you sure are doing a heck of a job, Brownie. George W. Bush always had a gift for saying the most inappropriately cheerful thing at the worst possible time:

> **"It's been a fabulous year for Laura and me."**
>
> —George W. Bush, December 12, 2001, three months after 9/11

Those who don't know their fabulousness are doomed to repeat it. Let's look carefully at the presidency of George W. Bush, so we can always remember how truly fabulous it all really was.

Our Shady Elections

And Our Illegally Appointed President

I was working late at *The Onion* office in Madison, Wisconsin, on November 7, 2000, watching the election on TV with our editor-in-chief, Rob Siegel. They declared Al Gore the winner. I exhaled deeply, feeling like the nation had just dodged a gigantic, falling boulder. Seeing Gore win was a huge relief, and I don't mean that in a small way. I mean it in a big way. It was like receiving the news that your possibly cancerous tumor was benign, not malignant; that the $35 million lottery jackpot was yours; and that the Green Bay Packers had just won the Super Bowl, all at the same time. It was an impossibly ecstatic moment, too good to last, a beautiful fairy tale that must be shattered by the hard fist of Texan reality. And then it happened . . . *the old switcheroo.* The face swap in the winner's box—did they really just do that to us? They showed the photo of Al Gore's well-fed and eminently reasonable face right there as the winner, while George W. Bush's face was so aptly marked "Loser." And then the switch—oh, the switch. Bush's smirking little goblin face popped up in the winner's box. I suddenly felt dizzy, presumably because of all the blood draining from my brain into my body's fight-or-flight instincts. I remember saying something along the lines of, "Fuuuuuuuuuuuuuck."

Rob and I locked up the office and took the elevator downstairs. We shuffled outside and heard cheering and loud music down the block. It was a Young Republicans victory party at a hotel. We stood outside, looking in on the gleeful, dancing Bush supporters. The women wore black business suits; some of the guys had taken off their blazers to really get down. One hooting GOP party animal had even loosened his tie. They arrhythmically pranced and stomped amid their red, white, and blue balloons scattered on the floor. Father, forgive them, for they know not what they do. I knew the party would be over soon, for all of us. The fun, frothy Clinton era had ended. Those Reagan/Bush years were back.

Ronald Reagan didn't become one of American history's most popular presidents because he reminded us of our friendly, cheerful grandpa. No, Reagan was popular because he was an extraordinarily talented politician with a natural ability to fool gullible people, and make them trust him despite massive evidence to the contrary. He was the conniving, power-mongering, money-grubbing Republican Establishment's wet dream of a leader. And no, the Republicans didn't just steal the White House for George W. Bush in 2000. Beginning in 1980, along with the unindicted leftovers of the Nixon administration, they invested years of innovative, backbreaking work and millions (billions?) of dollars into the development of a high-tech, criminal political machine so powerful and audacious, that by Tuesday, December 12, 2000 (with the Supreme Court's *Bush v. Gore* decision), they had succeeded in defrauding the American electorate right in front of our noses, in full color, on wide-screen HDTV.

The elections of 2000 and 2004 represented the apotheosis of the "permanent Republican majority" that was supposed to last forever (or maybe just a thousand years, like another permanent majority that comes to mind). This success was the result of a plan—a sly and devious plan, brilliantly inaugurated along with Ronald Reagan. How fortunate for us, then, that they should destroy themselves (as they destroyed Iraq's population and infrastructure) by picking Dubya to usher in the golden age of Republican rule. Few realized that frat-boy belligerence, tinged with Oedipal rage and brazen vulgarity, would result in multiple wars, global financial disintegration, and a previously unimaginable anti-Americanism that both threatens our sacred traditions of wanton consumption and exposes the neoconservative lust for worldwide military dominance for what it really is: penis envy.

"If we were a dog food, they would take us off the shelf."

—Representative Tom Davis (R-Va.) on the Republican Party,
New York Times, October 3, 2008

George W. Bush could have won the 2000 and the 2004 presidential elections the hard way. For example, he could have gained the support of the American people by using his sharp intelligence, his scrupulous honesty, his reassuring sagacity, his steadfast morality, his respect for human equality, his knowledge of world history, his insatiable curiosity, his humble nobility, his genius at compromise, his heartwarming compassion, his burning patriotism, his hilarious sense of humor, his "hipster cowboy" demeanor, his preppy sex appeal, and his utter devotion to Jesus Christ. After all, that's how he snagged his most devoted followers—people like Karl Rove, Condoleezza Rice, and Bruce Willis.

Thus he could have persuaded us to go to the polls in record numbers and vote him into office with a clear mandate to take over all three branches of our government for four or eight years so that he could do things his way, as a by-God rootin'-tootin' unitary executive—making richer the already-rich, spreading freedom for the great and good benefit of his campaign contributors, and establishing the United States as the only world military superpower, capable of crushing anyone, anywhere, anytime. If that's not what most people who voted for him had in mind when they cast their ballots, tough. They're not the Commander Guy.

George W. Bush could have tried to win both elections fair and square. Thank God he didn't have to. By November 2000, all the pieces were in place for an unimpeachable coup d'état. With the machinery of electoral fraud ready to go, our former head cheerleader was ready for his biggest pep rally ever. So what did that electoral machinery look like? It was a thing of beauty, just like Florida's secretary of state/Bush's campaign chairperson in Florida, the lovely Katherine Harris, the public painted clown face of the fraudulent vote count. She knew how to please her boss, none other than Jeb Bush, the governor of Florida, also known as George W. Bush's smarter but chubbier brother. Jeb Bush, Katherine Harris, and their minions had direct control over every vote cast in the state. They did everything they could to stop Democrats from voting, and once the election was over, everything they could to

Bush's Best Catchphrases

What slogans did George W. Bush constantly use to manipulate the dull-witted oafs of his electoral base?

1. "I will restore honor and integrity to the White House."

2. "We must stay the course in Iraq."

3. "We must fight the terrorists over there, so we do not have to fight them here at home."

4. "Freedom is on the march."

5. "Free cake for everybody."

6. "They hate us for our freedom."

7. "You're either with us, or against us. Also, I'm a uniter, not a divider."

8. "If a Democrat is elected president, America will be exposed to terrorist attacks. And I wasn't president on 9/11, that was some other guy."

9. "I will protect the life of the fetus, until it is eighteen years old and ready for combat duty."

10. "I'm a fiscal conservative. Don't worry, I won't bankrupt the country."

11. "Leave no child behind, except for those black kids stranded on the roof in New Orleans."

12. "I'm a compassionate conservative. Vote for me, or die."

Source: Bush's brain, Karl Rove

stop the counting of votes. The crimes (that's crimes, not dirty tricks) they committed are far too numerous to list, but here is a tiny sample:

Jeb Bush sent a letter with his signature, under the Florida State Seal, urging many Floridians to avoid hassle and vote using absentee ballots, regardless of whether or not they could make it to the polling place on Election Day. Florida law voids all absentee ballots submitted without a valid reason for voting by mail. Jeb was urging voters to break the law, and he knew their absentee ballots would be thrown out.

Katherine Harris knowingly purged nonfelon names from the rolls, and deliberately violated Florida's felons list statute by accepting 90 percent of the wrongly purged names found in 1999, and 80 percent of the wrong names in 2000, disenfranchising thousands of voters in traditionally Democratic counties. Harris illegally used her office as Florida secretary of state to actively campaign for Bush/Cheney; she approved the design of ballots that put some presidential candidates on a second page (the famous Pat Buchanan votes), which caused mass confusion among Florida's elderly voting population; she illegally failed to supervise the training of poll workers to assist voters; and in a shocking violation of conflict-of-interest laws, she expressed interest in being appointed as an ambassador by President Bush while she was busy obstructing the recounting of ballots.

Florida GOP operatives illegally altered 2,500 defective Republican absentee ballot applications, making them valid, and at the same time, they illegally ignored at least 550 Democratic absentee ballot applications. Republicans also submitted "handfuls" of absentee ballots in violation of a law that prohibits one person from submitting more than two absentee ballots other than those of a family member. In one case, an entire suitcase full of absentee ballots was submitted. Ten thousand "OptiScan-unreadable" absentee ballots were secretly duplicated in twenty-six heavily Republican counties in central and north Florida; the ballots favored George W. Bush by more than 2 to 1. Nearly all Florida counties failed to count "machine-unreadable" ballots where the voter's intent was obvious.

Republicans violated the National Voting Rights Act by providing broken voting apparatus to heavily Democratic minority districts, causing in some cases a "spoilage" and disqualification rate of up to 40 percent. Republicans illegally failed to provide voter assistance in Spanish and Creole, and ordered African-American citizens to "stand in the back of the line," causing them to leave the polls without voting. In

Spoiled Votes In The 2000 Bush/Gore Election

Total number of disenfranchised voters, divided by ethnicity:

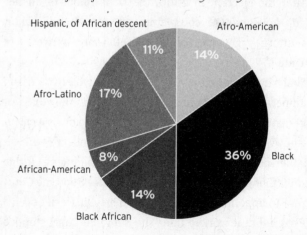

Source: Ex-Florida governor Jeb Bush's personal safe

23

heavily African-American and Democratic precincts in Miami/
Dade and Broward Counties, wide reports of prepunched
ballots were ignored. The compassionate conservatives also
prevented disabled citizens from voting.

During the seventy-two-hour window for requesting a
recount, Republican elections supervisor John Stafford told
the Gore campaign there were only 200 to 300 votes disqual-
ified, when there were actually 27,000. If he had not been
lied to, it is doubtful that Gore would have conceded without
a fight.

Supreme Court justices O'Connor, Thomas, Scalia, and
Rehnquist (who voted with the majority in *Bush v. Gore*) had
conflicts of interest because they were appointed to the court
by the father of George W. Bush—they should have recused
themselves. On December 12, 2000, the Supreme Court deliberately misrepresented the law by stating that electors had
to be chosen by December 12, when the true deadline was
December 18.

After the election in 2000, the Department of Justice
received *thousands* of complaints of voter fraud. Under
Bush's attorney general John Ashcroft, only twelve were
investigated.

That's a smattering of the documented voter fraud and
vote tampering in Florida in 2000. Anyone who can count, or
for that matter anyone who can't count but who owns a calculator, knows that Gore won Florida handily. And, of course, it
was Katherine Harris's certification of the fraudulent Florida
vote count that gave the corrupt United States Supreme Court
an excuse to appoint Bush to the presidency. It wasn't even a
good excuse, but it worked fine. The Supreme Court stopped
the hand recount in Florida, the most accurate way to count

votes, on the basis that such a count might cause "irreparable harm" to George W. Bush by "casting a cloud upon what he claims to be the legitimacy of his election." It used to be "our election," and we, the people, would determine who the legitimate winner was, by counting all the votes we had cast. Not anymore.

> **"You can fool some of the people all the time, and those are the ones you want to concentrate on."**
>
> —George W. Bush, spoken at a Washington, D.C., dinner, March 31, 2001

> **"It is my professional opinion that these numbers are fraudulent."**
>
> —Legal statistician Richard Hayes Phillips, PhD, in reference to Ohio's 2004 presidential vote count, from his deposition in the *Moss v. Bush* lawsuit, which reached the Ohio Supreme Court

Incredibly, Democrats stood by as the same thing happened in 2004. That election was all about Ohio, where the secretary of state in charge of elections, Ken Blackwell, was *once again* the co-chair of the Ohio Committee to Re-Elect George W. Bush. He promised to do everything he could to "deliver" Ohio to his snickering leader. Republican operatives removed voting machines from minority (Democratic) districts, and also tampered with registration cards and ballots. The GOP prevented more than 350,000 Ohio voters from casting ballots or having their votes counted. Voting totals favoring Bush in Ohio have been demonstrated by mathematical analysis to be statistically impossible. Official letters of deception were sent to tens of thousands of longtime voters informing them that they had been classified "inactive" and therefore ineligible to vote. A flyer distributed to Democrats informed them that they should not vote on Tuesday, November 2, but that they should vote instead on Wednesday, November 3. Exit poll data giving Ohio to John Kerry was retroactively corrected by the TV networks, just as they did in Florida in 2000. After the swipe was over, the ballots and election records from fifty-six of Ohio's eighty-eight counties were "accidentally" destroyed, in violation of a federal order to preserve them. This crucial evidence would have revealed conclusively that the election was stolen. It is unknown if the shredded ballots were used as confetti for George W. Bush's "victory" party.

And did you notice that whenever the Lie-O-Meter started dinging that terror bell at the top of the scale, George W. Bush got his way soon after? Bush used false terror alerts for political gains. Two days after the Democratic National Convention in 2004, Tom Ridge raised the terror alert level to "orange" for New York and Washington, based on three- to four-year-old intelligence. This false alarm destroyed the "bounce" that Kerry got in approval ratings after the DNC. And on Election Day, GOP election officials in Warren County, Ohio, cooked up a nonexistent terrorist threat to bar the media from monitoring the official vote count. The looming threat of al-Qaeda always seems to have a Republican face behind it.

As much as I'd like to credit George Bush Junior with figuring out how to steal elections, facts are stupid things. Honesty demands that we acknowledge the long and proud history of voter fraud, which goes back to before the ancient Greeks, whose innovations included trading sexual favors for votes. The Republicans' great contribution to early-twenty-first-century politics was to modernize voter fraud. They benefited from twenty years of painstaking experiment, trial, and error. They

From the Peanut Gallery

What are the most memorable quotes from President Bush's distinguished cabinet of henchmen?

Ari Fleischer–White House Press Secretary

"…all Americans… need to watch what they say, watch what they do."
—in response to comedian Bill Maher making a comment about 9/11; September 26, 2001

Condoleezza Rice–National Security Advisor, Secretary of State

"It did not warn of attacks inside the United States."
—describing a President's Daily Brief from August 6, 2001, titled Bin Laden Determined to Attack Inside the United States; *April 13, 2004*

Tom Ridge–Secretary of Homeland Security

"This war on terrorism is going to continue for an indefinite period of time."
—cheering up war, prison, and surveillance industries; October 30, 2001

John Ashcroft–Attorney General

"To those who scare peace-loving people with phantoms of lost liberty, my message is this: your tactics aid terrorists, for they erode our national unity and diminish our resolve. They give ammunition to America's enemies and pause to America's friends."
—transforming the Bill of Rights into terrorist ammunition; December 7, 2001

Donald Rumsfeld–Secretary of Defense

"We know where they are. They're in the area around Tikrit and Baghdad and east, west, south and north somewhat."
—lying his old, wrinkled ass off about Iraq's alleged weapons of mass destruction; March 30, 2003

Karl Rove–Deputy Chief of Staff

"As people do better, they start voting like Republicans—unless they have too much education and vote Democratic, which proves there can be too much of a good thing."
—a rare moment of candor; published in the February 19, 2001, issue of The New Yorker

Paul Wolfowitz–Deputy Secretary of Defense

"The most important difference between North Korea and Iraq is that economically, we just had no choice in Iraq. The country swims on a sea of oil."
—shooting down his earlier "The Iraqis will greet us as liberators" quote; May 31, 2003

Dick Cheney–Vice President

"It's absolutely essential that eight weeks from today, on November 2nd, we make the right choice, because if we make the wrong choice then the danger is that we'll get hit again, and we'll be hit in a way that will be devastating from the standpoint of the United States."
—warning of the impending catastrophe of a John Kerry presidency; September 7, 2004

"Go fuck yourself."
—to Sen. Patrick Leahy on the Senate floor about war profiteering by Halliburton; June 25, 2004

practiced on Bill Clinton. They attended Newt Gingrich's informative seminars. They carefully planned every aspect of the fraudulent victory, then struck at precisely the right moment and creamed the opposition's corn. And they did it with the delusional determination and belligerence that are the trademarks of Team Bush.

What did fair play ever get you? Do you know how difficult it is to win the U.S. presidency in a fair election? It may actually be impossible. Look at any of the historic squeakers: JFK and Nixon were so close, the election results weren't announced until noon the next day. Samuel J. Tilden led Rutherford B. Hayes by a mere 250,000 popular votes, but Hayes won more electoral votes, and the final results of the November 7, 1876, election were not known until March 2, 1877, just three days before Hayes's inauguration! Fairness be damned, George Junior learned early in life that the sweetest fruit is stolen fruit, which is comparatively easy to get, given his last name. And the well-stolen victory stayed sweet and juicy, despite megatons of clear, convincing evidence of fraud.

These are not your father's stolen elections, and I mean that literally. (Bush Senior's election took place a good twelve years before Junior's.) Ever since they outlawed tobacco, it's been impossible to run the kind of old-timey, smoke-filled back-room, ward-heeler, vote-the-cemetery, pay-as-you-go election that we used to know and love. All the fat politicians with their fat cigars and their squinting lackeys and buckets of beer and slimy phlegm-filled spittoons have nowhere to go anymore. Nothing will bring back the glory days when you could waylay a truckload of bums and drive them around from precinct to precinct, paying them a buck for each time they voted. Never again will a bootlegger like Joe Kennedy have the juice to call in a favor from the mayor of Chicago to deliver Illinois's electoral votes straight to his son's doorstep in Hyannisport. No, credit must go where credit is due—it was the Bush machine that taught the world how to steal an election the modern way.

And the best part is, they did it right out in the open where everyone could watch! It was a TV show, for chrissakes! You've seen the video of those bellowing Republican thugs breaking down the doors in Dade County, manhandling the ballots, twiddling the chads, then getting taken out for dinner by Katherine Harris. It was quite a show.

When Ronald Reagan got the ball rolling, he became the first president to try to drown the U.S. government in Grover Norquist's proverbial bathtub. He pioneered the now legendary Republican commitment, vital to George W. Bush's success, to dumb down American society by destroying the educational system. As everyone knows, well-educated folks are far more likely to choose the Democratic party over the Republican party. That's a sneaky way of saying, "Republicans are morons, generally speaking."

By 2000, there existed an entire generation of dumb citizens, ready and eager to believe lies, to hate their neighbors, and to vote against their own interests. The Republicans' revolutionary dumb down had worked like a charm. America was ready for a fascist coup, and George W. Bush looked like "the kind of guy you could have a beer with." Do you think this kind of man would even want to drink a beer with you, Joe Six-Pack? Do you think you're even remotely in his league? You could swap stories about your family, like how your grandpa used to take you fishin', while George could tell you how his grandpa used to go off to Nazi Germany to do some tradin'.

We were all so shocked and outraged when sad, old Vietnamese child-slayer John McCain and his frothing pit bull, Sarah Palin, tried to pin the label of "terrorist sympathizer" on Barack Obama. Isn't that what the Republicans have always done? They serve up an enemy that white, small-town America has never actually seen. With Michael Dukakis, it was Willie Horton. With Clinton, it was orally fixated Jewesses, suave European scamsters, and shady land dealers (sounds like a party). Reagan whipped his base into a frenzy by serving up the fantasy of "fat, black welfare queens" driving around in Cadillacs. Once George W. Bush had gotten through with us, of course, the enemy to link the Democrats to was terrorists. Bush has taken this whole charade into its endgame—the scary enemies that he will protect us against are burning for the desire to kill as many Americans as possible, without warning, and will even die themselves in order to do it.

We long for the innocent days of a good, old-fashioned rapist/murderer like Willie Horton. Republicans have always thrived by pushing the white-people-panic-button (nestled in the Caucasian brain between the fear of meeting a black person with the same last name as you and our memories of Kevin Costner's *Dances with Wolves*). They claim that their Democratic opponent is pallin' around with/paroling/giving money to these horrible enemies. And these enemies become terribly frightening boogeymen, as your typical Republican, white, small-town or rural voter has never even seen a black woman driving a Cadillac, a hardened al-Qaeda terrorist, or even a guy from Pakistan. Even the man who sells them their beef jerky and Marlboros looks just like them. You push that panic button, and boom, they're stabbing a Reagan/Bush/Quayle/Bush/Cheney/McCain/Palin sign into their lawn. Fear is the only tool the GOP has. The Republicans couldn't get *any-one* to vote for them if all they ran on was how badly they plan to screw us once they take office.

And now, eight years later, here we are. Were there electronic voting machines switching Obama votes to McCain? Of

Bush's Photo Ops

Never before has a soul so dark been bathed in so much golden light. What are President Bush's most memorable photo ops, what message did they intend, and what is the reality behind the image?

Bush's Photo	Message	Reality
Speaks at a warehouse, surrounded by boxes labeled "Made In USA"	"Strengthening America's Economy"—it's right there on the painted canvas backdrop	Actual "Made In China" logos stamped on boxes covered up with paper
Speaks at Mount Rushmore, framed level with giant president heads	Bush is a legend who will one day be immortalized in stone. Praise our mighty Pharaoh!	Bush can name only one of the four presidents on Mount Rushmore
Serves beautifully trimmed turkey to troops in Iraq on Thanksgiving	Even in a foreign combat hell-zone, American boys get their meat and potatoes	Bush dines and dashes, not sticking around for the mortar attack that evening
Peers down on devastated New Orleans after Katrina from window of *Air Force One*	Bush really cares, from 20,000 feet up	Bush is actually scoping out best new fishin' holes
Climbs atop pile of rubble at World Trade Center and speaks through a bullhorn	Whoever committed the murderous crime of 9/11 will be brought to justice	Bush did everything he could to stop a 9/11 investigation from happening
Bush's head ringed by an out-of-focus circular seal on far wall, creating a golden halo	Bush was chosen by God to lead our nation through these difficult times	God is busy designing a very special place in hell for George W. Bush

course there were. And, naturally, flyers were distributed telling Democrats to vote on November 5, the day after Election Day. The year 2008 was the first year that many states used new centralized voter registration databases, which are prone to error. Tens of thousands of registrations did not match existing voter records, and were therefore wrongly rejected. In Denver, after first blaming the post office, Sequoia Voting Systems admitted that it had not sent out more than 18,000 absentee ballots. In Ohio, 200,000 new voter mismatches became an issue that went to the U.S. Supreme Court. In Pennsylvania, a 2008 battleground state, posted notices told university students that those with outstanding tickets and warrants would be arrested if they came to the polls. The mayor of Indianapolis changed 31 polling locations without making any kind of announcement informing voters of the changes—citizens showed up at their usual voting place to find no voting machines. In California, a Republican scam told voters that they were signing a petition against child molesters, when the form actually switched their party registration from Democrat to Republican. And in the midst of a catastrophic mortgage crisis, Michigan's GOP threatened to use home-foreclosure lists to deny the vote to anyone no longer living at the address from which they were evicted.

Once again, I could go on for pages listing instances of voter fraud, intimidation, and rejection, all of them directed against Democrats. So, what happened in 2008? Surprise, surprise! The Democrats fought back this time. The same massive grass-roots movement that successfully solicited votes for Obama also created a network of poll watchers with the training and experience to nip problems in the bud. This time, we knew what to expect, and the brilliant Republican plan no longer worked. So much for the Republicans' "permanent majority." With the Republican party in complete disarray, one has to wonder, will they figure out new and effective ways of keeping Democrats from voting in 2012? Or will we have a window of time that can be used to truly govern America, and to provide the protection and the services only our government can provide? They say these are cyclical trends, so let's be thankful that we lived to witness the end of the Reagan Era, twenty years too late to do any good for the environment, the educational system, the health care system, or for American diplomacy. We've been given an opportunity to start over, start fresh. Let's not screw it up, like that guy who's clearing brush in Crawford, Texas, right now.

> **"I know millions of Americans will be overcome with pride at this inspiring moment that so many have waited for, for so long."**
>
> —George W. Bush, on the approaching inauguration of Barack Obama,
> CNN, November 5, 2008

OUR MANY WARS

If You Thought the U.S. Was Bad
Under Bush, Try These Countries

A t the dawning of the golden new millennium (that would be the year 2000, Before Bush), the United States stood unchallenged in the world. Our military, technology, economy, and culture was unparalleled in its advancement and influence across the globe. The world's economic systems ran on the computers, Internet, and software that we had created; Britney Spears and *The Matrix* were hot worldwide; Russia was locked in the bathroom with a jug of vodka; and no one wanted to mess with our M1A2 Abrams battle tanks or AH-64 Apache attack helicopters. The almighty dollar made the euro look like funny money from a board game, as all currencies that are printed in pink should be. We were like the ancient Colossus of Rhodes, a godlike figure staring out over the oceans, secure in our supremacy. In 2008, it is clear that the Bush administration reared its head as the Kraken to our Colossus, using a multitude of slippery

tentacles and claws to tear down the power of America, sending chunks of it crashing into the waves below. The wars in
Afghanistan and Iraq are two of the thickest and most powerful tentacles of this monstrous horror from the deep. The
wars of George W. Bush have dealt huge and lasting damage to the United States military, the wealth of the nation,
the people of Iraq and Afghanistan, and our international
status in world opinion. Especially in Iraq and Afghanistan.

Some may choose to take a favorable view of Bush's
foreign policy, saying that he was shocked into vigilance by
9/11, and vowed to never allow another horrible attack like
that again. This led to his swift decision to invade Afghanistan
less than a month later. The problem with that perception is
that the United States had positioned troops in Tajikistan to
invade Afghanistan months before 9/11, and even told other
nations' governments about its planned attack on the Taliban
in June 2001. MSNBC reported that detailed Afghanistan
war plans were on President Bush's desk, ready to be signed,
on September 9, 2001. Bush was not shocked into action
by 9/11; the plans and means to invade Afghanistan were
ready to go. You can't mobilize the equipment and supplies
for an aerial bombing campaign and a full land invasion on
the other side of the world in less than a month. As for Iraq,
those who believed Bush when he said that we must dis-
arm Saddam Hussein of his weapons of mass destruction
were in fact deceived by fraudulent evidence and calculated
lies. The most likely explanation as to why Bush would
want to invade two countries, as evidenced by his previous
retarded-prisoner executing, condemned-inmate-mocking
and childhood-amphibian-torturing, is that he's an aloof
elitist, insulated from the real world by power and privilege,

whose eager yet careless use of power is accompanied by no concept of the human suffering that wars unleash.

"Fuck Saddam. We're taking him out."

—George W. Bush, to three U.S. senators in March 2002, one year before Iraq invasion (from *Time* magazine, March 23, 2003)

Yes, the senators did laugh uncomfortably at Bush's remark. No governmental or military professional wants to be exposed as a neocon nerd playing a big game of Risk. The problem with Risk is that the game never ends—you have to stay up all night playing, you have to constantly replace the armies that just died, and sooner or later someone is going to get angry and slam his fist down on the board in disgust, destroying everything. The American taxpayer has also been holding up this extremely expensive game of Risk for more than sixty years now, with 6,000 bases stocked with half a million troops in more than 130 countries worldwide, and our arms are getting tired.

The reason that Bush gives us for why we're fighting in Afghanistan and Iraq is September 11, 2001. That terrible day saw the most grandiose, sophisticated, highly destructive terror attack in our nation's history, apparently catching the U.S. military defense network completely off-guard. But where have the terror attacks been since then? 9/11 seems obviously to be the act of a criminal terror network that is frighteningly innovative, horrifyingly effective, and terrifyingly motivated. But since 9/11, America has suffered no serious terror attacks on the homeland with a note left on the rubble reading "From al-Qaeda." How motivated is this sinister global terrorist syndicate we've all heard so much about? There has been none of the major-league al-Qaeda threats that they warned us about—no dirty bombs, no biological or chemical attacks, no truck bombs, no attacks on nuclear reactors, no anthrax (ah, so that *was* a U.S. government scientist who mailed that out after all). Is the threat from al-Qaeda sufficient enough to warrant the massive mobilization of two foreign wars?

Or perhaps al-Qaeda has us ensnared in their master plan. Osama bin Laden himself gloated in his October 29, 2004, video that Bush's invasions of Iraq and Afghanistan were a great gift to al-Qaeda, making it easy to attack American troops. Osama cackled over how America's strength was being drained away in Bush's foreign wars, and urged Americans to vote for Bush to keep the wars going. Red-blooded American patriots rose up to this evil terrorist mastermind . . . and obeyed his command. Bush opened up a six-point lead over John Kerry in the first poll after Osama's video aired. Predictably, al-Qaeda wanted us to vote for John McCain as well. Al-Qaeda Young Republican clubs are now springing up in madrassas from Cairo to Jakarta. No girls allowed! Okay, Sarah Palin can come, as long as she wraps those killer gams in a burka.

The home front on terror is quiet, but since Bush launched his Global War on Terror, terrorist attacks have shot upward around the globe. It got so bad that Condoleezza Rice canceled the publication of *Patterns of Global Terrorism,* a State Department annual report, after it embarrassingly showed that there were more terrorist attacks in 2004 than in any year since 1985. However, bombs going off in Iraq are not terror attacks on the United States homeland. Those are attacks aimed at our occupying army, and given everything we've done to Iraq, is it really all that surprising that we're being met with armed resistance? You know, what with the Iraqi civilian casualty count being over one million and all. Our own country was founded out of guerrilla warfare against a foreign army. It's not hard to imagine young Iraqi guys sitting around watching their own bootleg VHS tape of *Red Dawn* and getting pumped up over it, too. There's also the terrorist violence of the Iraqi civil war between Sunnis and Shia Muslims. Wouldn't it have been nice if Bush had told us what he had planned back when he was running for president on the campaign trail? Bush could raise his fist and say, "My fellow Americans, I promise to drop our nation into the middle of a vicious, age-old conflict between two desert-dwelling tribes over who Muhammad's real son was." The crowd cheers.

Emboldened by the United States' overwhelming power when he first seized office, Bush had an unquenchable lust to use that power, and a staggering level of incompetence to go along with it. Given these attributes, a constant state of war suited him just fine. It's just too bad that Bush couldn't have been president for more than eight years. We really could have experienced a war that would last our lifetimes. Nothing centralizes power to the state like war, and nothing quells criticism and dissent like it. Bush loved every minute of it. Plus, his floundering incompetence would have ensured that the war could have gone on forever. It seems that our battle plan in Iraq and Afghanistan is to fly a helicopter around and wait to see who shoots at it. We encourage foreigners to embrace their inner terrorist, so that we may then kill them.

"I just want you to know that, when we talk about war, we're really talking about peace."

—George W. Bush, Washington, D.C., June 18, 2002

"We're kicking ass."

—George W. Bush, on the security situation in Iraq, to Australian Deputy Prime Minister Mark Vaile, Sydney, Australia, September 5, 2007

Did Bush really think that an illegal invasion would lead to a free Iraq and a model of democracy in the Middle East? Perhaps, but we'll leave that for George to fantasize over as a comforting dream, tucked away in his 1,000-thread-count sheets while trying to fall asleep at night with the blood of more than one million dead people on his hands. The real meaning of Bush's doctrine of preemptive war is that "international law does not apply to us." Bush has no respect for laws. He disenfranchised voters. Regulations on financial fraud—did away with those, too. The idea that natural resources belong to sovereign nations—nope, your oil is ours, and we're taking it. Not recognizing international law is a free license to loot and plunder. Those Americans who supported Bush on Iraq thought that they were on the winning team—who cares if the Iraqis got a taste of our big-stick policy? George W. Bush is the winner, and he's on our side! Actually, he's not. Those who supported Bush's Iraq heist didn't realize that the looting and plundering that Bush committed against Iraq would also be turned on them. Jobs are being lost, investments are dropping like hot rocks, wages are down and overtime is up, while Bush's wars consume $4,750 *every single second*—and the meter is still running, my friends.

Remember that fifteen of the nineteen alleged 9/11 terrorists came from the kingdom of Saudi Arabia. But of course, we couldn't offend the Saudis by bombing the hell out of them. Bush engages in lengthy make-out sessions with Saudi princes and prances merrily at their traditional all-male sword dances. He has close and intimate contacts with many influential Saudis that go back for years. In fact, Bush has done everything he can to promote medieval Islamic fundamentalism in the Arab world. It's obvious if you look at the economic situation realistically. What is more preferable to the Anglo-American elite: modern, nationalist, secular, democratically elected Arab leaders who want to use their country's natural resources to improve life for their impoverished and growing populations, or iron-fisted, limb-amputating kings who keep their people oppressed and the oil tap flowing? Better yet, how about some mumbo jumbo fundamentalist clerics who want to turn their backs on modernity and fragment their countries into a patchwork of ethnic and religious rivalries? Let them squabble over who loves Allah more while Exxon pumps out their oil. The Anglo-American alliance has always undermined or assassinated nationalist leaders in the Middle East, like Mohammed Mossadegh in Iran, Gamal Abdel Nasser in Egypt, and yes, Saddam Hussein, who did have Iraq running as a modern country before we blew it up, albeit with the thumbscrews cranked on tight. Bush's attack on Iraq even gave birth to a brand-new Islamic terror organization: al-Qaeda in Iraq. Simple but catchy. He helped out al-Qaeda with some new recruits, along with promoting Osama bin Laden into a world-famous celebrity and making sure he wasn't brought to justice, dead or alive.

So how did Bush treat our heroic troops, the grunts whose job it is to make Bush's geopolitical fantasies a reality? "Like shit" would be the short answer. Just five miles from the White House lies the Walter Reed Army Medical Center, a hospital intended to receive wounded troops from Iraq. Back in 2005, it was revealed that the hospital was filthy and falling apart, but Bush had other priorities. His Pentagon appointees had lobbied Congress against funding military pensions, health insurance, and benefits for widows of veterans—Rumsfeld wanted that money to spend on new military hardware and recruiting instead. So the Walter Reed hospital was turned over to IAP, a private company with no experience in military medicine, headed by former Halliburton executives who had overcharged the United States in Iraq and trucked ice all around the country on the taxpayer's bill instead of driving it to New Orleans after Hurricane Katrina. The president of IAP who landed the $120 million Walter Reed contract is in fact named David Swindle. The staff of three hundred at Walter Reed had already dropped to sixty, who were fired and replaced by fifty private workers. In 2007, the *Washington Post* reported: "Behind the door of Army Spec. Jeremy Duncan's room, part of the wall is torn and hangs in the air, weighted down with black mold. When the wounded combat engineer stands in his shower and looks up, he can see the bathtub on the floor above through a rotted hole. The entire building, constructed between the world wars, often smells like greasy carry-out. Signs of neglect are everywhere: mouse droppings, belly-up cockroaches, stained carpets, cheap mattresses." Welcome back from Iraq, boys. Those prosthetic legs should be coming next month for ya.

Our troops are not superheroes. There's only so much they can take. Not to say they're not heroes—of course there's a lot of dragging-your-wounded-buddy-to-safety stories out there—but they are not true Marvel/DC spandex-style *super*-heroes. It would be great if U.S. Army soldiers all had the intelligence, strength, speed, and invisibility of the entire Fantastic Four, but unfortunately, they're normal kids thrown into an impossible situation. Clifton Hicks, a tank driver, Humvee .50-cal gunner, and infantryman in southern Baghdad in 2003 and 2004, describes this situation perfectly: "We're not bad people. We were there because we thought it was the right thing to do. We were there because we thought we were going to make things better. We were there because we thought these people wanted us to be there. And then you show up and you realize, that there's a whole bunch of people there that want to kill you. And guess what, they look just like the folks who don't want to kill you. So, are you going to sort them out and figure it out? The only way to ensure your survival is to make sure that you put them in the dirt before they put you in the dirt."

Bush sent our troops into free-fire zones, no friendlies, game on, weapons free. Infantryman Steven Casey describes his convoy of vehicles driving down a highway in Iraq the wrong way, and any vehicle that was driving toward them on the correct side of the road was fired upon. He speaks of massive civilian casualties and, in some cases, orders to inflict those casualties. They killed everything and everyone who dared to show themselves—mostly civilians who were trying to escape the battlefield. This is what happens when a conventional force such as the U.S. military attacks a densely populated urban area.

An oft-mentioned emotion that veterans of all wars face is that civilians don't understand—they have no idea—of what war is really all about. These people who surround them every day, who have never experienced combat, will never truly understand what life was like for these veterans. Chest-beating, flag-waving, belligerent loudmouths who have never been shot at or watched their best friend's legs get blown off must be particularly difficult for veterans to deal with. It's too bad that one of those guys has been commander-in-chief for the last eight years, whose idea of military duty was securing a clean cup of some other guy's urine to pass his flight physical exam in the Texas Air National Guard. Bush certainly was the out-of-touch, clueless, yet demanding "Boss From Hell" for U.S. troops, but a stressful day at work means something entirely different to military personnel.

Up to 50 percent of returning soldiers report symptoms of psychological disorders, but the military's mental health system is woefully inadequate to treat them. U.S. soldiers have been billed by the U.S. military for damaging equipment. For the first several years of Bush's wars, troops were nailing scrap lumber to the sides of their underarmored Humvees to protect themselves against roadside bombs. The military is overstretched, with troops facing extended tours of duty and being "re-upped" for combat after they have already fulfilled their combat-duty requirements. We have just about the entire National Guard and Army Reserve forces, the guys who signed up for one weekend a month, deployed in foreign combat zones. And taking photographs of flag-draped coffins filled with young American boys (and now girls, too) as they are returned to U.S. military bases is still banned. It's hard to keep recruitment levels up when your target audience sees the guy they would be replacing coming home in a coffin. Bush had to make sure that his supply of cannon fodder would keep flowing.

The only sign that U.S. troops are being killed, for those of us who have the luxury of not being military families, is the half-raised flag at a local Perkins restaurant. At some point, in many communities, the Perkins manager figured it would be just as easy to leave the flag in a permanently half-lowered position, instead of cranking it up and down every few days. If only America's kindly yet rage-driven grandpa, John McCain, could have raised the giant star-spangled banners of our Perkins restaurants once again, so that we may watch it flap triumphantly on high while we enjoy our Steakhouse Scrambler and fresh-baked Mammoth Muffin. That bottomless cup of coffee is a lot more fun when you don't have to think about a dead eighteen-year-old American while drinking it.

But Bush wanted those eighteen-year-olds, bad. He even wrote a law so he could get to them more easily. Buried within the 670 pages of the No Child Left Behind Act, Bush's education law passed in 2002, is a requirement for public schools to provide military recruiters access to school facilities and contact information for every student. If the recruiters don't get what they want, the school faces a cutoff of all federal aid. Yes, they're coming for your kids. You see them sometimes, the military recruiters in baggy, dust-colored uniforms and desert boots, lurking outside sub sandwich shops and pizzerias, with clipboards and patriotic smiles. Why do they need your children so badly?

> **". . . economically, we just had no choice in Iraq. The country swims on a sea of oil."**
>
> —Deputy Defense Secretary Paul Wolfowitz

The fact is that the oil is sitting right down there in the ground, and that is wealth just waiting to be taken. And Bush won't let Saddam Hussein jerk the price of oil around, either—that might shave off 1 to 2 percent of Exxon's and British Petroleum's yearly profits. There will be no support for clean alternative energies, and the oil companies will fight tooth and nail against them, because they know they've got wealth that is already established, just waiting to be dug up. It doesn't matter if people are slaughtered, cities are destroyed, or the atmosphere is blackened, because goddamn it, that is pure money down there! The idea of just letting that oil go, a long-term decision for the good of the world, is unthinkable to these kinds of people. Instead, Bush dreamed of what could be the largest untapped source of that oil wealth, the sparkling Caspian Sea, flowing into his hands via a pipeline laid across Central Asia, through the lovely land of Afghanistan.

THE AFGHANISTAN WAR

"The most important thing is for us to find Osama bin Laden. It is our number one priority and we will not rest until we find him."
—George W. Bush, September 13, 2001

"You know, I just don't spend that much time on him [Osama bin Laden], to be honest with you. I don't know where he is. I truly am not that concerned about him."
—George W. Bush, March 13, 2002

It's almost disappointing to consider Bush's abandonment of the effort to capture bin Laden, purely from the perspective of enjoying shocking, fascist, Grand Guignol, geopolitical theater. He really could have given us more of a show. Imagine the bluster and threats, the daring psy-op exploits through the mountains of Afghanistan that we could have been entertained by for a full eight years, with the incredible action-movie climax capture of Osama bin Laden at the end of 2008. Bush had the most compelling mission statement in Afghanistan imaginable—capturing those he claimed to be responsible for the attacks of 9/11. He promptly dropped that mission and sloughed off on the job, like the D student that he was. Afghanistan was just a warm-up for Bush. He bombed the country, declared victory, installed the well-dressed U.S. puppet Hamid Karzai as president, forgot to reconstruct the country after destroying it, and rolled up his sleeves to deceive the American public about his next war. Now Afghanistan is once again in a downward spiral, and it all comes full circle. As it was in 2001, so it is now.

Our president explained the invasion of Afghanistan as retaliation on the Taliban for not turning over Osama bin Laden. It's not like the Taliban was hiding the big O under their bed. According to ABC News Australia, they had actually offered to extradite bin Laden to any country of the United States' choosing, a full year before the 9/11 attacks. After 9/11, the Taliban responded to U.S. threats by offering bin Laden in exchange for proof that Osama was involved in the attacks. Bush didn't have time for such a trivial matter. Besides, FBI Director Robert Mueller admitted that the FBI had no hard evidence connecting bin Laden to 9/11 and no legal proof on the true identities of the suicidal hijackers of 9/11, so you can see why Bush would ignore the Taliban's ridiculously logical request. Bush had no proof to tie bin Laden to 9/11. Even Dick Cheney backpedaled on their "Osama did 9/11" line on March 29, 2006, stating on the Tony Snow radio show, "So we've never made the case, or argued the case that somehow Osama bin Laden was directly involved in 9/11. That evidence has never been forthcoming." Wow. Is Cheney playing Jedi mind tricks on us? Of course, they *did* argue that Osama bin Laden was the mastermind of 9/11, in order to justify their invasion of Afghanistan. Bush and Cheney lie to us to make us forget how much they lied to us. It's easier that way, they can get right back to clearing brush and fly-fishing, instead of dealing with some war-crimes hoo-hah.

Besides, U.S. troops and planes were already positioned in Tajikistan, and the war plan was waiting to be signed. Bush was ready to let 'er rip. The world's richest country, the United States of America, would invade the world's poorest. The neo-con cabal hanging out in the basement of the Pentagon were bursting to put some new plastic army pieces on their map of Central Asia, surrounding Iran. The population of Afghanistan was over 50 percent orphaned children under the age of fif-teen years old, widowed women, and fragile elderly. And after all, these Afghans had denied us our trans-Asia-pipeline deal. Bush wanted to get in on the Caspian Sea, touted as having more oil reserves than Saudi Arabia, and pipe the oil south, avoiding Iran, through Afghanistan to Pakistan and India. We had even romanced the Taliban, speaking in a language they could understand, huskily: ". . . accept our carpet of gold, or we bury you under a carpet of bombs." Yet the deal fell through. A month later, bombs were dropping on Afghanistan. When Bush can't pay off some third-world junta, they are dead meat. That is one transgression that Bush will not forgive—him not being allowed to give brutal foreign dictators huge U.S. Treasury checks.

So what happened to the pipeline? It never happened, because the Taliban still control the southern half of the country. Nothing's been built. How about the buzz on the gigantic untapped oil of the Caspian Sea? That's looking a little more Tony Mandarich by the day, with initial estimates being criticized as severely inflated and unrealistic. Once again, Bush comes across as that guy at work who always talks about the incredible projects he's got cooking, but then never actually produces anything. "Oh, you mean that marketing strategy I was working on? With the blimp, the fireworks display, the one thousand Chinese acrobats, and the herd of elephants? Yeah, that never quite came together. But let me tell you about my next plan . . ." The difference is that your co-worker just makes you do extra work to cover for his ass. The result of Bush's huge risks, which he casually discards, is hundreds of thousands of people dead and national infrastructures pulverized.

Even when we had Osama bin Laden cornered in the mountains of Tora Bora, with 1,000 of his number-two lieutenants, Bush didn't get the job finished. He was able to mobilize 2,500 Afghan fighters, led by double-crossing warlords, who were supervised, cajoled, and bribed by forty U.S. special forces troops. These elite warfighters passed out $100 bills to the Afghans to capture bin Laden for them. Unsurprisingly, it turned out that the Afghans had no interest in being shot at any more than they normally are, and watched bin Laden escape while counting their money. Where is the motivation, Bush? You wrote this script, you have to own your part. Or is your whole drama a farce, and Osama bin Laden worth more to you alive than dead?

Even though Bush conveniently forgot what he was supposed to accomplish in Afghanistan, we haven't slacked off on bombing the hell out of this war-ravaged nation. Is this the best way to deal with poor, starving regions awash in weapons, warlords, tribal enmities, and armed violence—to attack them with overwhelming military force, to set the troubled country even more on fire? Afghanistan has been in a state of war for a solid thirty years now, first with Russia, then with itself, then with us. The entire nation has been reduced to rubble. When you see photographs of Afghan fighters, they look so miserable, squatting in their rags up on cold mountain peaks. These mujahideen look cold, hungry, and chapped. Maybe these guys just need someone to invite them in for a hot bowl of oatmeal, listen to their problems, find out why they're so angry. Do we need to jump headfirst into their culture of blood vows and revenge killings?

In interviews with Taliban fighters, Canada's *Globe and Mail* newspaper found that their main reason for fighting the Americans is that Americans are killing their families. What if we took away that reason? That is an action that is actually within our power, unlike hunting down every single terrorist on the planet before they reveal themselves. What would happen if we admitted that Bush's war was bullshit from the beginning and we "cut and ran" from Afghanistan? The

Doing the Math

When it comes to bombing civilians in Iraq and Afghanistan, let's keep it simple, George. Here are two mathematical proofs, the inherent logic of which should be apparent to anyone who survived grade school.

Many U.S killings of civilians		No U.S killings of civilians
+ More resentment from civilians	**OR**	+ Less resentment from civilians
= More attacks on U.S. troops		= Less attacks on U.S. troops

Which result did you prefer, Commander-in-Chief?

British did exactly that, a hundred years ago when they got their asses handed to them by the Afghans, and Britain is still around—sipping tea, eating Weetabix, and watching footie. There have been no recorded instances of Afghan resistance fighters swimming over to Britain to attack them.

Is hunting down nomadic mujahideen through the rugged foothills of Central Asia really a viable strategy to fight the threat of domestic terror attacks? Are these the guys we have to worry about—impoverished tribesmen who are completely alienated and isolated from the modern world? Or is it guys who know English, high-level encryption software, and the security measures at airports and nuclear plants and who possess the ability to send and receive e-mails? Maybe we should just lock up anyone who wears glasses and knows what the word *Google* means. If we stopped bombing these hinterlands, packed up, and went home, would all of these poor, starving tribesmen suddenly transform into James Bond, able to outwit security at airports, thwart NORAD, and fly commercial airplanes into skyscrapers? It's doubtful that they could even find the bathroom at an airport. Would they start cooking up weapons-grade anthrax over their campfires? No, only U.S. Army scientists at Fort Detrick know how to do that. It's hard to see these illiterate, poverty-stricken people having the technological expertise and international savvy to really do anything. Afghanistan is a broken land that hasn't had a functioning government since Alexander the Great.

Meanwhile, our attacks on Afghanistan have merely chased the evil bearded ones out of their traditional stomping grounds and into neighboring Pakistan, where they take pot shots at U.S. troops and then escape across the border. The United States is now chasing al-Qaeda into Pakistan's

Federally Administered Tribal Areas, or FATA. (It's too bad the word *Land* wasn't added onto the end of FATA; it would have made the acronym perfectly self-explanatory.) It's just like how we bombed Laos and Cambodia in order to chase down those slippery Viet Cong. We are a gigantic, lumbering bear, pawing at a swarm of mosquitoes as they flit away across the steppes of Central Asia. The problem is that Pakistan is a sovereign country with a very twitchy military, which has already shot at U.S. helicopters, forcing them to turn back. Now we're attacking with unmanned Predator drones. After all, that's a rough neighborhood over there! The FATA is no place to be for good American boys, might as well send in the killer robots. How many countries will we bomb in this wild-goose chase? And besides landing beefy contracts for Bush's well-connected private military-contractor-company campaign supporters, what's the point of it all?

Well, there's always the standard way to track progress in this business—the body count. Eight thousand Afghans were killed in 2007 alone, and the UN reports that civilian casualties have jumped by 39 percent in 2008. The killing has mostly been accomplished by aerial strikes. The general mind-set of the U.S. military seems to be that if you've already spent the $575,000 on a Tomahawk cruise missile, you might as well use it. A popular target that U.S. commanders believe are al-Qaeda powwows turn out to be wedding parties or funerals. Fifty to one hundred people gather in a village for a few days to celebrate a wedding or mourn a loss together, and we strafe and bomb them with AC-130 gunships while they're sleeping. When U.S warplanes strafed the village of Chowkar-Karez in 2001, killing at least ninety-three civilians, a Pentagon official said, "The people there are dead because we wanted them dead." His reason was that all ninety-three of those people were supposedly Taliban sympathizers. When asked about the Chowkar-Karez incident, Rumsfeld replied, "I cannot deal with that particular village."

Bush even bombed Red Cross warehouses in Afghanistan filled with relief goods, setting them ablaze. So we're not buildin' schools and spreadin' freedom, as Sarah Palin chirped in her vice-presidential debate? No, we're killing children. It's too bad Palin didn't appear in a town hall–style debate where a real question could be asked, such as "Governor Palin, have you ever looked at this photograph showing dead Afghan children killed by American bombs, lined up in rows on the ground like limp produce at some cannibal farmers' market? As a mother, how does this photo make you feel?"

The body count is Bush's only real accomplishment in Afghanistan, because the reconstruction of this desperate land never happened. The United States actually omitted any humanitarian aid to Afghanistan in their 2003 budget. In October 2008, America's sixteen intelligence agencies warned that Afghanistan was on a dangerous "downward spiral" into violence and chaos. It is now the fifth least-developed nation in the world—a one-position drop from 2004. Approximately half of the population cannot afford enough food to guarantee bare minimum health levels. Many will starve this winter. Unemployment is as high as 80 percent. Kabul, originally designed for about eight hundred thousand people, now holds more than four million, mainly squeezed into crumbling shacks without electricity or safe drinking water. The roads are cratered and crumbling. And even though Bush spends $36 billion a year on this war, only 5¢ of every war-dollar goes toward aid to Afghanistan. Out of this tiny slice, a full

40 percent returns to donor countries in corporate profits and salaries. The rest is given to private reconstruction companies who don't actually build anything.

One mission of our troops in Afghanistan that could be admired around the world would be to protect Afghan women from Afghan men. Under the Taliban, women were stripped of all rights—denied schooling, the right to work, or to move about freely. They could walk the streets only if accompanied by a male relative. Female doctors, lawyers, and other professionals couldn't practice their crafts. Women were blocked from receiving health care, as only men were allowed to practice medicine, and male doctors were banned from touching female patients. (Really? You can't touch a woman, even to save her life? Jesus Christ, what a bunch of fucking fags. The bad kind of fags, not the good kind.) For violating these rules, women were beaten in the street with sticks by Taliban soldiers, the same guys whom we have been allowing to regroup. Ladies, go easy on your man the next time he doesn't put the toilet seat down. Just be thankful that you weren't born in Afghanistan.

It's a terrible cliché to write "put the women in charge," but in all seriousness, Afghanistan is a country that is in dire need of an injection of feminine energy. Hundreds of Afghan women immolate themselves every year, with cooking oil and a match, because their men treat them so badly. Presumably Bush could have found the money in his $36 billion budget to fund a program that would have created jobs and social support for Afghan women. We could have enhanced schools, by actually building them and paying for their teachers. Can we still get an early-learning program going that would teach little Afghan boys how to interact with Afghan girls in ways that don't involve throwing rocks at them? Perhaps Barack Obama will wage his smarter war in Afghanistan. He could air-drop in Gloria Steinem and a grizzled platoon of NOW paratroopers to educate and advance Afghan women.

Whatever approaches we take would be better than the current U.S. military strategy of random bombings and zero reconstruction. If Obama wants to fight this war, our commandos should actually go in to capture or kill Taliban leaders, instead of just calling in an air-strike on the entire village. Throwing more fresh-faced recruits from Small Town, U.S.A., into an escalated land war in Afghanistan is probably not the best plan for anyone involved. Their Pashtun language skills are just not very good. They didn't pick up the finer points of Afghanistan's tribal systems in high school geography class. They are not equipped to improve Afghanistan's gender relations, foster schooling, or convince the Taliban that art and music are an integral part of the human experience. They are equipped to kill people, especially at long range, and they can't even explain why they're doing it.

The members of the Revolutionary Association of the Women of Afghanistan (RAWA) brave mortal danger to support one another and to make the plight of Afghan women known to the world. With video cameras smuggled in under their burkas, they have filmed public executions of Afghan women in packed soccer stadiums. When a woman from RAWA, who is living in exile in Pakistan, was asked if she wanted to return to Afghanistan, she said this: "I miss Afghanistan very much, it's my country. I love my city and my country a lot. I am a fugitive here. Whenever there is peace in Afghanistan we will never go to another country. We will go back to rebuild Afghanistan and experience good days, I hope." This is the kind of person who will help fix the devastation of the U.S.–Taliban war, and this is the kind of person we should support.

THE IRAQ WAR

"You know, one of the hardest parts of my job is to connect Iraq to the War on Terror."

—George W. Bush, in an interview with CBS News' Katie Couric, September 6, 2006

As opposed to his neglect in Afghanistan, Bush embarrassed himself and his country with his brutal and moronic eagerness to invade Iraq. Publicly, his administration employed all the logic and justice of a lynch mob in their rush to war. You can almost imagine George turning to his partners, Dick, Rummy, and Cletus, to shout, "Hey, boys, did you hear? A buncha fig-munchers just blew up the goddamn World Trade Center! Let's go roast us up some Arabs! Hey, there's some there right now, in Iraq! Kill 'em all!" The last sentence of Bush's exact quote might have actually been "Bring 'em on," but you get the idea.

Or did Bush's bluster distract us from the final execution of a long-term strategy of engagement in the Middle East? Saddam was a ruthless, psychopathic tyrant, which is why he was such a perfect asset for the CIA. Back in 1959, the CIA hired Saddam Hussein to kill the president of Iraq, Abd al-Karim Qasim, who was guilty of anti-American crimes such as trying to nationalize foreign oil companies in Iraq and decriminalizing the Communist party. Saddam failed in his assassination attempt, but the CIA liked the cut of his mustache. A CIA-organized coup in 1963 did kill Qasim, and Saddam's Baath Party took power. Young Saddam was put in charge of Iraq's secret police, so we supplied him with the names of thousands of communists, leftist activists, and community organizers. You can guess what happened next. We wrote the "to-do" list for Saddam's first torture and killing spree.

Throughout the 1980s, Reagan, Poppy Bush, and Rumsfeld showered Saddam with weapons—helicopters, howitzers, bombs, anthrax, cyanide, mustard, and nerve gas—to enable him to keep on killing, especially if he used them on the Iranians. The CIA taught him how to use poison gas weapons during the Iran–Iraq War, the same ones that he used on his own Kurdish population. His worst crimes occurred when we were arming and supporting him. With our weapons and encouragement, Saddam's invasion of Iran in 1980 led to the deaths of well over a half-million Iranians and Iraqis. Saddam also killed 300,000 of his own people from 1979 to 2003. That's horrendous. More than one million Iraqis have been killed since the U.S. invasion over the last six years. What's the word for that?

This long-term strategy of engagement began with the support of Saddam Hussein against Iran, continued with the double-cross when we promised not to intervene in Kuwait before Hussein invaded in 1991, then finally culminated in the invasion of the country after we had starved it with sanctions for twelve years. We set up Saddam, then took him down. Our engagement continually escalated, from covert support, to open weapons trading, to limited war, to sanctions, and finally, to a full-on invasion that's been quite profitable for select U.S. companies with ties to the president. Bush stayed the course, continuing down this disastrous path that began with the meddling of the CIA. We're at the end of the road now, without even our handpicked brutal dictator to run the show for us in the Middle East. Now it's down to American kids, walking the streets of Baghdad with a sweaty grip on their M-16s. It's awfully convenient to say that the only kind of government that works in the Arab world is one with an iron fist. That's the only kind of government we've ever allowed them to have. "They love the iron fist! LOVE it! We need to send in three hundred thousand troops now, they love it so much."

But in order to fulfill their long-term strategy for catastrophe, Bush and his team back in 2003 needed *some* kind of a reason to invade Iraq. They decided to make one up.

"The British government has learned that Saddam Hussein recently sought significant quantities of uranium from Africa."

—George W. Bush, making a claim he knew at the time to be false, State of the Union Address, January 28, 2003

". . . for reasons that have a lot to do with the U.S. government bureaucracy, we settled on the one issue that everyone could agree on: weapons of mass destruction."

—Deputy Secretary of Defense Paul Wolfowitz, explaining the U.S. rationale to invade Iraq, *Vanity Fair* magazine, April 2003

Iraq sure did have a lot of weapons of mass destruction back in early 2003. Oh yeah—big time. Serious death-ray stuff. Biological, chemical, nuclear, and radiological. They told us about it constantly. We were warned about Saddam's uranium turning into mushroom clouds over our own cities. Colin Powell went to the United Nations to wave fuzzy photographs of blob-shaped Iraqi "chemical munitions bunkers" and hold up a small glass vial of imitation anthrax powder, intoning in his best Doctor Doom voice, "With the powder in this vial, I can kill everything in a ten-mile radius." Iraq had even unmanned aerial vehicles that could fly across the Atlantic Ocean to rain down horrendous poison-bombs on our East Coast. It was going to come down to them or us, UAVs or SUVs, freedom or terror. Bush got much of this high-level phony-baloney intelligence information from the greasy Ahmed Chalabi, an exiled Baghdad elitist and convicted criminal wanted for bank fraud who hoped to lead Iraq. The information was all completely bogus, but was served up as rock-solid horse shit to the American public.

Why do politicians lie to us? Why do they scare us with stories about weapons of mass destruction, or the fiction that we're going to liberate a people by committing mass slaughter against them? Are we all so romantic that we need to be seduced into a war? What if Bush had come out and said, "Yeah, it's about the oil. We're going to invade another country, to control their oil supply. Probably will have to kill a lot of people, but hey, they got oil that we want. Let's roll." Would Americans object all that much? Or would we finally rise up and shout, *"Goddamnit, will you fuckers start developing solar power already?!?"*

While trumpeting the dangers of Iraq's nonexistent WMD, the Bush administration was defeating efforts to gather information on the true situation in Iraq. Let us raise a toast to Bush's retribution against outed CIA agent Valerie Plame Wilson, a scandal which displays the Bush

Texas-Sized Yarns

Given his devotion to terrifying the American people, President Bush initially proposed more exaggerated claims of Iraq's WMD programs, which were subsequently toned down by his advisors.

Official U.S. Claims of Iraq's WMD	Bush's Proposed WMD Claims
Chemical weapons	Chemical weapons that melt your face off
Biological weapons	Biological weapons that rot your balls off
Nuclear weapons program	Gamma weapons program to develop an Iraqi Incredible Hulk
Mobile bio-weapons labs	Mobile bio-weapons labs disguised as ice cream trucks, prowling the streets of America to sell your children smallpox sundaes with rainbow jimmies
Uranium from Africa	Uranium from *darkest* Africa (accompanied by audio of pounding jungle drums)
Aluminum tubes to be used for uranium-enriching centrifuges	Aluminum tubes to be used for the molestation of your daughters
Anthrax	Anthrax . . . in your mailbox!!! Oh wait, a U.S. government agent actually did that
Unmanned aerial vehicles capable of bombing the U.S. East Coast	Unmanned subterranean vehicles capable of erupting out of the ground to disgorge hordes of cannibalistic mole-men in major American cities

administration at its most treasonous. Bush persecuted Americans who were actually looking for and telling the truth about our safety. The crime was senior White House officials—Karl Rove, Dick Cheney, and his toady, "Scooter" Libby—revealing the identity of Valerie Plame Wilson as a CIA agent. She was an undercover CIA operative in its Counterproliferation Division, in charge of finding evidence to back up Bush's assertions on Iraq's WMD. The reason that Bush's hit men exposed Plame Wilson is that her husband, Joseph Wilson, had criticized Bush's false claims that Saddam Hussein had procured uranium from the African country of Niger. Mr. Wilson happened to be the ambassador to Niger, and had been sent there to investigate Bush's tall tale. When Wilson reported that there was no uranium coming out of Niger, he exposed Bush as a liar. So Rove and Cheney clumsily retaliated against Joseph Wilson by revealing his wife's secret identity to conservative columnist Robert Novak, who printed it in his widely syndicated column. By exposing Valerie Plame Wilson, Bush's goons not only endangered her life, but also the lives of scores of other intelligence operatives around the world with whom she was in contact. The exposure disrupted long-term, real efforts to track and control loose WMD across the globe. Let the record state that Bush, this "national-security president," chose to betray national security and endanger U.S. agents in order to politically smear those who dared to expose his lies.

> **"The same folks that are bombing innocent people in Iraq were the ones who attacked us in America on September the eleventh."**
>
> —George W. Bush, Washington, D.C., July 12, 2007

> **"See, in my line of work you got to keep repeating things over and over and over again for the truth to sink in, to kind of catapult the propaganda."**
>
> —George W. Bush, Greece, New York, May 24, 2005

All the lies, the smears, the British "sexed-up dossier" on Iraq's WMD, and the mysterious "suicide" of Dr. David Kelly, a British weapons expert who had expressed deep concerns over the British and American case for war, added up to what was planned all along—Operation Iraqi Freedom, achieved through the carpet-bombing of Iraq. The shock and awe reached a thrilling climax five weeks later, on May 1, 2003, with George Bush's "Mission Accomplished" costume party aboard an aircraft carrier. What if Bush had actually gotten our troops out of there when he appeared on the aircraft carrier? We could have chalked up a "Dubya" in the win column and gone home. But no, Bush flew in on the backseat of a warplane and hopped out wearing a military flight suit. Our victorious action figure modeled for the cameras, with his awesome helmet and oxygen-mask accessories. Many have commented that the bowlegged, big-eared, squinty-eyed, smirking Bush looked like Ham the Astrochimp in his jumpsuit on the flight deck. It must be added that this chimpanzee-like appearance was enhanced by a tightly strapped flight harness, which created a noticeable naked-chimp–style bulge in Bush's frontal groin region. The world's alpha male was on full display. Genuflect before his divinely stuffed codpiece!

"Major combat operations in Iraq have ended. In the battle of Iraq, the United States and our allies have prevailed."

—George W. Bush, beneath his "Mission Accomplished" banner, aboard the USS *Abraham Lincoln*, May 1, 2003

It was his finest hour for this lifelong cheerleader—first cheering on the fellows at all-male Andover prep school, then clapping in the stands at Texas Rangers games, then pumping up Republican pep rallies across the nation, and now this. Bush was ready to get into that flight-suit costume, buckle those straps up under his crotch, make a big entrance, and put on a show. Huge banners and flags, sailors in their crisp white uniforms, all the pomp and pizzazz. The military band played a Muzak version of "We Will Rock You" by Queen, minus the Freddie Mercury vocals, as Bush strode to the podium, pumping his fist in the air. The war was won, proclaimed Bush beneath his star-spangled victory banner, bathed in the golden sunlight shining upon the newly liberated-from-the-threat-of-tyranny waters a few miles off San Diego.

It was easy to laugh at Bush on the aircraft carrier; it was all so supremely campy in its macho posturing. Yet that moment was also truly chilling. Everyone who had opposed the war, and the idea of war in general, felt so defeated. Once the laughter died, there was a cold, gnawing horror that perhaps *this is the way it's going to be* from now on. Bush looked triumphant, in an easily understood, cartoonlike way. It seemed that at least 51 percent of Americans were loving him in that flight suit, and the elections were coming up. Perhaps Bush would reign eternal, a warrior king ruling a Valhalla on Earth. Perhaps shock and awe really did work miracles. They made the indiscriminate bombing of a defenseless civilian population look as wholesome and satisfying as apple pie. Casualties were relatively low, and we were told that both wars had been won. Perhaps we'll invade Syria next. *Perhaps Bush was right.* The *Project for the New American Century* seemed to be unfolding exactly as planned, and no one knew how far we would go to fulfill its full-spectrum-dominance destiny.

But the world righted itself again. The sun still rose, the

sky was still blue, and of course, war remained a tragedy. Bush only gave the illusion of competence on that aircraft carrier. He proved to be infinitely better at photo ops than running foreign wars and reconstructions. It is doubtful that Bush regularly shops at stores with signs that read, "You Break It, You Buy It." Instead, his mantra in Iraq has been "You Break It, You Fuck It Up Some More." In the lead-up to the war, the Bush gang was like a raving pack of children before Christmas, who just couldn't wait to open their big Iraq present. Once morning finally came, the Bush kids tore open Iraq, but then didn't know how to assemble their new toy. So they threw a temper tantrum and burned the whole house down.

Bush's postwar plan to govern Iraq seemed to be to throw the country into as much chaos as possible. U.S. troops did nothing to stop the looting of Baghdad's schools, universities, hospitals, libraries, and food-distribution centers in the aftermath of the invasion, choosing only to protect the Oil Ministry building. They even encouraged looting. Sweden's largest newspaper, *Dagens Nyheter,* published an interview with a Swedish man of Middle Eastern ancestry who had gone to Iraq to serve as a human shield. Khaled Bayoumi said, "I happened to be right there just as the American troops encouraged people to begin the plundering." He described how U.S. soldiers shot security guards at a government building, then "blasted apart the doors to the building." Next, according to Bayoumi, "from the tanks came eager calls in Arabic encouraging people to come close to them. Arab interpreters in the tanks told the people to go and take what they wanted in the building."

U.S. troops watched while the National Museum in Baghdad, home to priceless antiquities from the dawn of civilization, was systematically ransacked by professional

President Bush's Greatest Moments—May 1, 2003

U.S. Department of Defense

The full presidential package swoops in to announce
that our mission in Iraq is accomplished.

SPC Ronald Shaw Jr., U.S. Army/Department of
Defense Visual Information Center

The mission of Operation Drive Around Iraq and Get Blown Up
by Hidden Bombs continues.

art thieves. These people knew exactly what they were looking for, passing up gypsum copies for the real treasures.
The records of the museum, an international hub of archeo-
logical research, were burned, making it impossible to even
catalog what was lost. Millions of artifacts disappeared into

the lucrative and illegal international trade in antiquities. The looting of Baghdad served to rob and burn down what was left of the city's infrastructure, so that private U.S. companies like Halliburton could be given huge contracts to pretend to rebuild it all, for which they overcharged.

Apparently forgetting that Iraq was a one-party state under Saddam, Bush fired everyone in Iraq who was a member of Saddam's Baath political party. The leaders of the army, the police, and an entire government of civil servants and teachers were suddenly unemployed, broke, and desperate. Bush also dissolved the Iraqi army, putting 400,000 men who were trained to kill out of work. Brilliant move, George. This de-Baathification predictably led to the bloodbathification of Iraq, giving unpaid soldiers nowhere to go but the insurgency. Bush even left Iraq's ammunition dumps wide open for them. The security was so bad that tens of thousands of tons of guns and ammunition were plundered from unguarded arms depots, fueling Iraqi resistance and weaponizing Iraqi sectarian conflicts. Violence exploded across the country.

Besides helping to instantly create a large, violent, armed force of guerrilla enemies, Bush's viceroy in Iraq, L. Paul Bremer III, managed to mysteriously lose up to $9 billion of Iraq reconstruction money through financial fraud and corruption. Bremer's Coalition Provisional Authority (CPA) that ruled Iraq was a rogue operation, unauthorized by the U.S. Congress, and its accounting was "off the books." There were unlimited opportunities for financial theft, by U.S. government officials and contractors, entrepreneurial Iraqis, and anyone else around. For example, Halliburton charged the CPA for 42,000 meals for soldiers while in fact serving only 14,000. Contractors played football with $100,000 bricks of shrink-wrapped $100 bills. Out of a package of $12 billion in U.S. cash sent to the CPA, $9 billion is unaccounted for. Yes, they were driving trucks filled with your money out of Iraq.

Bush and his neocon henchmen dreamed of exploiting Iraq's natural resources to the fullest within a completely deregulated corporatist state. Iraq would be a gleaming capitalist utopia in the desert: labor unions suppressed, the media controlled, and corporations freed to chase profits without laws or limitations. The empire of Enron would rise again in the golden sands of Mesopotamia. Bush brought his experience bankrupting Texas oil companies to this challenge of a new corporate Iraq, which predictably went down in flames. Bush took our tax money to enrich a small elite of U.S. companies/his campaign donators like Halliburton, Bechtel, and Blackwater, as well as any other crooks that could steal their share. How did it work out for the rest of us, without such an exclusive stock portfolio? More than 4,000 dead American soldiers, over 1 million dead Iraqi civilians, Iraq separated into tribal enclaves, 4.7 million Iraqi refugees, and even an increased price of oil, along with the inestimable karmic debt that we have brought upon ourselves with the maelstrom of terror, death, and poison that we have unleashed upon Iraq.

To keep us pumped up for his roaring meat-grinder, President Bush produced plenty of Hollywood-style action movies, with a lot of special-effects magic behind the scenes. There was Pat Tillman, the square-jawed linebacker who left an NFL career to die serving his country in Afghanistan while fighting off a Taliban ambush—except he was actually shot in the forehead three times by a fellow U.S. soldier, possibly at close range. Bush lied about Tillman's death, even to his own grieving family, so he could use Tillman, a photogenic pro athlete, as a military recruiting tool. There was Jessica Lynch, a U.S. soldier who bravely fought off Iraqis "like Rambo" who were attacking her convoy, suffering bullet and stab wounds, until she was captured, raped, and sodomized by the dastardly terrorists, but then rescued in a daring U.S. Special Forces raid—except she actually didn't fire a shot in combat, was not harmed by the Iraqis, was injured in a vehicular accident, and was recuperating nicely with special treatment in an Iraqi hospital when the U.S. commandos stormed in, firing blanks and setting off explosions for their camera crew. Two days before Delta Farce busted up the hospital, the Iraqi doctor who was treating Lynch had in fact tried to return her to the U.S. Army in an ambulance. But American troops opened fire on the ambulance with Jessica Lynch inside, forcing it to flee back to the hospital. There was the pulling down of the Saddam statue by the jubilant Iraqi masses—except there were only a few dozen Iraqis who were probably paid to be there, and a U.S. armored vehicle pulled down the statue anyway. There was the incredible capture of Saddam, achieved by a brilliant stroke of U.S. tactics—except Iraqis had tipped off the Americans, who brought their camera crew along to film their big moment. And finally, there was Saddam's December 30, 2006, execution by hanging (Merry Christmas, everybody), captured on grainy cell-phone video, when it seemed like Bush had run out of money for special effects. That should have been the Republicans' pièce de résistance, their main event, their summer smackdown, but it was a grim and grimy anticlimax. If there's one thing you expect Bush to get right, it's an execution.

It was one of those many moments of the Bush years that makes you laugh while your eyeballs roll back into your skull—Saddam was taken to a playset actually named Camp

Scorecard for the Iraq War

Key Issues	Mar. 19, 2003	2009	Grade
U.S. troops killed	0	4,300 or so, we're told	F
Terrorist attacks in Iraq	0	Lost count a while ago	F — an A for the terrorists, though
Projected cost of Iraq War	Only a few billion	$2 trillion. Note the *t* in "trillion."	F, as in "our failing economy"
Price of oil	$25/barrel	$87/barrel	F, as in "WTF?"
Saddam Husseins	1	0	B-. His execution was terribly anticlimactic.
Iraqi WMD	Millions, according to Rumsfeld's wet dreams	Zero. Mission accomplished!	A for effort
S. Hussein posters	10,572,348	Zero. BOO-YAH!	A+
Sectarian violence in Iraq	None	Shitloads	F for the Sunnis, A for the Iran-backed Shias
Concrete blast walls in Baghdad	Four, around Saddam Hussein's compound	Miles and miles and miles and miles...	A+ for those who miss the Berlin Wall
Radioactive depleted-uranium ammunition fired in Iraq	300 tons, from 1991 Gulf War	2,300 tons	A+ for cancer and genetic mutation
Rape rooms	27	Classified by order of the U.S. Defense Department	A+ for rape enthusiasts

Justice to be hanged. He was captured in Operation Red Dawn—as in the cheesy 1984 flick with Patrick Swayze, where the U.S. is invaded by the Soviet Union and a group of resistance fighters, the Wolverines, takes their high school's sports mascot as their name. And back in the "real" world, Saddam Hussein was in fact captured by Wolverine Teams 1 and 2. Does the American leadership who thinks up these names still play with their G.I. Joe toys?

"There are some who feel like that the conditions are such that they can attack us there. My answer is bring them on."

—George W. Bush, on Iraqi insurgents attacking U.S. forces, Washington, D.C., July 3, 2003

Thanks for answering the question, George. Good luck hunting down Cobra Commander and Destro. Bush really did have a great time playing at being a war president. He got to beat his chest, issue threats to many nations, drop tons of bombs, and pose for photo ops in front of lots of supercool army guys. Bush would get all serious once in a while when it was time to deceive the nation, but once that mission was accomplished, he was able to let loose and just have a good chuckle over how easily he fooled us into a war:

"We found the weapons of mass destruction. We found biological laboratories. . . . And we'll find more weapons as time goes on. But for those who say we haven't found the banned manufacturing devices or banned weapons, they're wrong, we found them."

—George W. Bush, Washington, D.C., May 30, 2003

"Those weapons of mass destruction have got to be somewhere! Nope, no weapons over there . . . Maybe under here . . ."

—George W. Bush, joking about his failure to find WMD in Iraq while narrating a comic slideshow during the Radio and Television Correspondents' Association dinner, Washington, D.C., March 24, 2004

Gosh, where *did* that reason our soldiers are dying for go? While Bush cracked up the assembled journalists—the same people who swallowed one steaming dung pile after another on Iraq's WMD, then dutifully wrote and printed it—a slide show included photos of Bush peeking under furniture in the Oval Office. "Nope, not here either!" The journalists laughed appreciatively and uproariously at our hilarious president's stand-up routine. But if Bush had really wanted to kill out there, he should have shown a sped-up clip of a U.S. Humvee driving down the road in Iraq when it hits a roadside bomb and young Americans' severed limbs fly through the air, all set to the tune of Benny Hill's rollicking theme song "Yakety-Sax." That gets a laugh every time.

Along with well over four thousand dead American soldiers in Iraq (and it's a safe bet that this number has been massaged with some Fannie Mae–style accounting), over one million Iraqis are dead as a result of violent conflict since the U.S. invaded. How does this death toll explain the puzzling Iraqi response to Operation Iraqi Freedom? Let's use the power of our imagination to get a feeling for why Iraqis have been resisting the American occupation. Let's create an alternate history in which the Babylonian Empire never crumbled, and that on March 20, 2003, the superpower nation of Iraq invaded the United States of America. To keep it proportional, let's say twelve million Americans were violently killed over the last six years. New York City, Washington D.C., and Los Angeles are shattered ruins, the crumbling streets drowned in lakes of raw sewage. Denver was besieged by the Iraq Army with white phosphorus bombs, incinerating thousands. Iraqi snipers shot at ambulances trying to rescue the wounded. High-rise apartment buildings in Chicago with people living inside were strafed by Iraqi gunships, while Iraqi soldiers sat on adjoining rooftops and watched the show. Electricity and running water are rare commodities in U.S. households. Iraqi troops stage raids on our suburban ranch houses in the middle of the night, smashing through the front door with guns to take away American men and teenaged boys to torture them at an Iraqi-run prison in Dallas. Our daughters and wives are raped and killed by marauding Iraqi soldiers. Unexploded Iraqi cluster bombs are littered across the United States, killing our children who stumble across them. To get to our jobs, we must pass through checkpoints where if we don't slow down and obey everything that is being barked at us in Arabic, there's a good chance that we'll be riddled with machine-gun fire. Would this life inspire you to wave a cheery hello to the Iraqi soldiers you pass by every day on Main Street? Or would it motivate you to kick their fucking asses at any chance you got?

"I would still invade Iraq, even if Iraq never existed."
—George W. Bush, in a remark made to the Long Beach *Press-Telegram*, August 21, 2006

Usually in war, those who are the targets of such violence can at least take some small comfort in the idea that one day the war will end, and a new generation in the future will not have to endure such horror. French, Russian, and Vietnamese children are all able to skip and play in the sunshine, blissfully ignorant of the realities that once occurred at the Somme, Stalingrad, and Hué. We have taken even this small comfort from the Iraqis. One aspect of the freedom that Bush has brought to Iraq is the freeing of Iraqi DNA to grotesquely mutate through his use of depleted-uranium ammunition. This waste product of the nuclear energy industry is 60 percent as radioactive as natural uranium. Depleted uranium is also twice as dense as lead, so it is widely used by the U.S. military—they've fired three thousand tons of it into Iraq during Bush's invasion. The army loves the heavy, high-impact DU shells because they are also self-sharpening and pyrophoric, meaning they pierce tank armor then burst into flame inside. When a DU shell hits, it explodes in a burning spray of radioactive dust, which can contaminate wounds and be inhaled. The DU dust scatters across the land, whichever way the desert winds are blowing. Geiger counter readings at sites in downtown Baghdad record radiation levels one thousand to two thousand times higher than normal. The radioactive shelf-life of depleted uranium is 4.5 billion years.

Iraqi, Afghan, and Serbian children (remember those?) live and play among radioactive debris. Cancer rates, child leukemia, and birth defects have all been soaring upward in Iraq since Poppy Bush first used depleted uranium in 1991 (he really was a wimp, though, he only used 320 tons of DU, while W. has shot 3,000 tons, as noted above, into Iraq and 1,000 into Afghanistan by now). There has been a dramatic surge in severe birth deformities among Iraqi children. So, how to paint this picture . . . do you know *Fangoria* magazine? Um, it's like that. Freakish horror-movie creature-shop nightmares made real. Yes, President Bush made Mesopotamia—the cradle of our human civilization—a radioactive wasteland. Talk about shitting in your own bed.

There is also no selfish comfort in thinking that depleted uranium is a burden that only those foreigners will have to deal with. U.S. soldiers who were stationed in Iraq are having children born with the same horrendous birth defects. They're also deathly ill. Herbert Reed is a formerly healthy Iraq War veteran who believes depleted uranium made him sick. It takes him ten minutes to swallow all of the pills he has to take, including morphine four times a day. Deborah Hastings of the Associated Press reports on Mr. Reed's condition: "Since he left a bombed-out train depot in Iraq, his gums bleed. There is more blood in his urine, and still more in his stool. Bright light hurts his eyes. A tumor has been removed from his thyroid. Rashes erupt everywhere, itching so badly they seem to live inside his skin. Migraines cleave his skull. His joints ache, grating like door hinges in need of oil."

When poisoned by DU, the uranium replaces the calcium in your body, so your teeth literally crumble. You know those teeth-falling-out nightmares, the worst kind of nightmares, the ones that are so real that you frantically check your still-intact teeth with relief in the morning? Yeah, Bush dragged that foul beast up from our collective id and into the bright light of reality, kicking and screaming. This is the globalization of war—drifting clouds of radioactive metallic microparticles that slip right through the most heavily guarded borders on windy days, future children of soldiers in foreign lands being born poisoned and deformed due to the dust a parent is inhaling today. Given the radioactive decay rate of depleted uranium, it's clear now that Dick Cheney was right, and that Bush's war will *not* end in our lifetimes. We all breathe the same air, whether we support or oppose the Iraq War, and we can't hold our breath waiting for this war to end. Enough damage has been done, it's time to put this fire out now.

WHO ELSE WANTS SOME?

"I don't care if it [the Iraq War] created more enemies."

—George W. Bush, interviewed in *War Journal: My Five Years in Iraq*, by Richard Engel

Although there is no real exit plan for Iraq or Afghanistan and we have constructed huge and permanent bases in both countries, Bush did his best to kick off two more wars before he flew off to his retirement ranch. Syria was raided by U.S. commandos in helicopters on October 27, 2008. Bush said that we killed an al-Qaeda smuggler, while Syria said we also killed ten innocent construction workers who happened to be in the line of fire. It is unknown if Bush had a pack of playing cards with photos of hunky construction workers on them that he gleefully crossed out. We're also now on a regular schedule of bombing Pakistan with Predator drone missile strikes—possibly killing some terrorists, probably making some new ones.

Unfortunately, using our killer robot planes to attack this huge Muslim nation that has both nuclear weapons and a fragile government is one Bush policy that Barack Obama does not hope to change. We're just lucky that Bush didn't pull out the big guns on Iran, saving Obama from yet another gigantic, bloody mess to clean up. However, Bush always kept up his pressure on the Persians, lying about their nuclear weapons program even though a National Intelligence Estimate, from all sixteen U.S. intelligence agencies, stated that Iran has no current nuclear weapon program and it is doubtful if they intend to pursue one. Bush did try to conjure up a Gulf of Tonkin–style hoax in January 2008, involving Iranian speedboats attacking U.S. Navy ships in the Persian Gulf, to get the war party started. He spliced a spooky phone call of someone saying "you will explode" into a video of the ships routinely passing each other in international waters. Yes, Bush went down swinging, all the way to the end of the twelfth round.

Even though Bush maniacally threw punches left and right throughout his eight-year blitzkrieg, he still lost the fight that he started. The Iraqi Shia won their 2006–2007 war against the Sunnis, and now control three-quarters of Baghdad and a majority in parliament. This Shia dominance in Iraq increases the influence of Iran in the country, as Iran is also Shia. It is amazing, George, that you somehow used the power of the Great Satan to strengthen the Islamic Republic of Iran. The Taliban is on the rise in Afghanistan. Pakistan is becoming increasingly destabilized. Hamas now has majority leadership in the Palestinian legislature, and Hezbollah is surging in Lebanon (the flag of Hamas shows crossed swords, while Hezbollah's features an AK-47). Kim Jong-Il is putting a glorious paint job on his freshly hatched nuclear missiles in North Korea, although he may have gotten too excited over his new nukes and had a stroke. Bush intervened in Somalia with U.S.-trained and -funded Ethiopian troops to fight a moderate Islamist militia, but now the country is in chaos and the Ethiopians are about to withdraw. When that happens, the Bush-backed Somali government is expected to fall. Bush also armed, trained, and advised the army of Georgia, hoping to build yet another pipeline. He backed Georgia for NATO membership, then whistled while it invaded South Ossetia, a breakaway region with a large Russian population. Putin stomped on that effort, demolishing the Georgian military, the pipeline plans, and the possibility of Georgia joining NATO. Bush succeeded only in making Russia stronger, another amazing Bush contribution to our favorite enemies, considering the dismal state of Russia during the 1990s. Ronald Reagan must be spinning in his grave.

Thinking of Reagan always brings up the notion of dying in an apocalyptic nuclear war. Bush carried on this tradition, threatening to use "bunker-buster" tactical nukes preemptively, on nonnuclear states, in his War on Terror. After a decade of restraint, Bush dramatically increased the U.S. nuclear weapons budget. He has continued to pursue the unworkable and fantastically expensive "Star Wars" missile defense system (don't you realize that the more you tighten your grip, Bush, the more star systems will slip through your fingers?). This is not simply a defensive shield; the system includes killer satellites in space. One weapon the Pentagon is developing is the Hyper-Velocity Rod Bundle, nicknamed "Rods from God." These would be 220-pound tungsten bars that are fired from an orbiting satellite, hitting the earth at 7,200 mph, with the force of a small nuclear weapon. Wow, Bush really *does* want to build the Death Star. Back on terra semi-firma, Bush continued to provoke Russia by placing "defensive" nuclear missiles in Eastern Europe. Didn't we get a little twitchy when the Reds were slipping nuclear missiles into Cuba? Yes, the Risk game continues to go on, late into the night. Bush kept on losing pieces under the couch, but he insisted on playing until he won.

You can almost hear Bush saying, "We've got to win. We have to stop these terrorists." Do you really need a 220-pound tungsten bar fired from outer space to stop a guy with a box cutter? Were all one million of those Iraqis whose lives you stopped terrorists? It just makes you want to point Bush toward our Declaration of Independence. He can skip ahead to the second paragraph: "We hold these truths to be self-evident, that all men are created equal, that they are endowed by their Creator with certain unalienable Rights, that among these are Life, Liberty and the pursuit of Happiness." Did you understand that part about "all men," George? Iraqi, Afghan, Pakistani, and Syrian children have just as much of a right to live as American children. It's the self-declared original purpose of the United States of America, so you should have followed the rules, you fucking troglodyte. Instead, you cheated, started wars based on lies, and got what you deserved—a pair of shoes whipped at your head by an Iraqi reporter. But of course, you ducked. You always ducked. But now you don't have to worry about any more tough questions or footwear flying at you. You rode off into the sunset like a cowboy, atop your riding lawnmower, in endless looping circles around your dusty ranch. It will just be you out on the range now, left alone to think about what you've done. That tear in your eye? Don't worry, George, it must just be all that brush you're kicking up. Try not to cry too much.

HIS RELAXING
VACATIONS

Bush Puts the R&R in War on Terror

No matter how bad things got during his presidency, George always seemed to have his shoes off, his feet kicked up, and his ass on vacation. While the rest of us panicked and agonized over terrorism, war, natural disasters, and our faltering economy, Bush really enjoyed his downtime over the past eight years. Our fake president sure did love his fake ranch: holding press conferences on its dry, dusty road, where he looked like a tough cowboy with a big belt buckle ready to dispense justice; getting all hot and sweaty clearing brush with his Secret Service bodyguards; or just spending a quiet Texas evening dry-humping his mechanical rodeo bull out back.

I confess that there is no confirmed source for the mechanical bull rumor. But consider Laura Bush, speaking at the White House Correspondents' Association dinner on April 30, 2005, telling a joke about George on his ranch: "George didn't know much about ranches when we bought the place. Andover and Yale don't have a real strong ranching program. But I'm proud of George. He's learned a lot about ranching since that first year when he tried to milk the horse. What's worse, it was a male horse." Damn. It's humbling to realize that I could never be as nasty as Laura is to her own husband. George's supporters really have deserted him, when even his own wife says that he jacks off big, meaty horse cocks until they jizz all over him. Hey, whatever helps you unwind.

"I would say the best moment of all was when I caught a seven-and-a-half-pound largemouth bass in my lake."

—George W. Bush, on his best moment in office, in the German newspaper *Bild am Sonntag*, May 7, 2006

Bush is now on permanent vacation, thank God, and the numbers of his total vacation days during his presidency are in. Our vigilant leader spent 487 days chilling at Camp David and 490 days relaxing at his ranch in Crawford, Texas. Let's get out the calculator here . . . a total of 977 vacation days, divided by eight years at 365 days each . . . yeah, that's 33 percent of Bush's entire presidency spent at just these two getaway spots. For a guy who constantly told us that our enemies could attack at any time, Bush sure did skip out of work a lot. Children in elementary school have a more grueling yearly schedule than Bush did. It's by far the most vacation time ever taken by a president—the record-holding presidential vacationer was formerly Ronald Reagan, another fake cowboy, but at least one who had made it as a professional actor.

"Spending time outside of Washington always gives the president a fresh perspective of what's on the minds of the American people," White House press secretary Scott McClellan once told reporters. "It's a time, really, for him to shed the coat and tie and meet with folks out in the heartland and hear what's on their minds." Too bad for Bush, that included heartland folks like Cindy Sheehan, the peace activist whose son was killed in Iraq. Sheehan camped out on the road leading to Bush's ranch, squawking that she wouldn't leave until he agreed to interrupt his vacation and meet with her. He didn't.

Bush also tried to enjoy the longest presidential retreat in more than three decades, a two-month stay at his ranch, before it was rudely cut short by Hurricane Katrina on August 25, 2005. Bush had already been chilling, Crawford-style, for over a month. He was way too busy riding his mountain bike on this one kick-ass dirt hill to do anything about the detailed damage forecasts that Homeland Security officials had sent him two days before Katrina drowned New Orleans, which predicted that the city's levees might be breached. After fitting in a guitar lesson and dropping off a birthday cake for John McCain in Arizona while New Orleans went all Mad Max, Bush finally did leave vacation early to deal with Katrina. However, he told us all that we owed him, big-time. Then in 2006, Cindy Sheehan bought five acres near Crawford, which she plans to use as a base for future protests when Bush is in town. What a drag. Where can George get away from it all?

Don't feel too sorry for Bush; he had all kinds of cushy vacation spots around the world. Besides the Western White House in Crawford, Texas, there was the Middle Eastern White House in Dubai—a palatial five-story penthouse with real diamond floors atop a 3,000-foot tower in the shape of a scimitar, staffed with a docile and nimble staff of child camel-jockeys. There was also the Offshore Tax-Shelter White House, located in the beautiful Cayman Islands of the sparkling blue Caribbean, where Bush wore colorful Hawaiian shirts and received many international businessmen in suits and ties, who arrived in powerful motorboats with several hulking assistants holding chrome briefcases. And there was the Subterranean Nuclear Bunker White House, located beneath an undisclosed mountain somewhere in North America, where Bush enjoyed driving a golf cart and throwing rubber bouncy balls down the cavernous concrete hallways.

It's a little-known fact that Bush used up his eight-year presidential allotment of sick days within his first three months in office. There were prolonged stretches of half-days, when Bush said that he needed time to work on "his own personal projects." Our president was also on a seasonal schedule of taking off on summer Fridays, winter Mondays, spring Wednesdays, and fall Tuesdays. You can understand why Bush held hardly any press conferences—the least amount of any president since the invention of television. It's not just that Bush didn't want to be challenged or held accountable for his actions, it's because he really hated getting out of his sweatpants and having to put on a shirt and tie for everybody.

Many have seen the video clip of George W. Bush wearing a polo shirt on a golf course in front of reporters, calling on all nations to stop the terrorists. "Now watch this drive," says Bush as he lifts his golf club and takes his swing. It's hard to top this moment for Bush as the ultimate asshole boss who enjoys some fun in the sun after giving his underlings the most difficult work imaginable. "Okay, team, there's people out there who want to kill all of us, but we have no idea who they are. Your job is to find out who they are before they actually commit their crimes and kill everyone. I'll be out golfing the rest of the week, so I won't be reachable. See ya, suckers!" You have to think that Bush's attitude inspired the asshole bosses of the world to emulate this ultimate asshole move. Bush got a bunch of other guys to do his work for him while he went golfing, with many of them becoming terribly wounded or even dying in order to get the job done. This executive behavior set a real example for all of the fine leadership at Fannie Mae, Freddie Mac, Bear Stearns, and Lehman Brothers to follow over the last few years, and look where we are now.

Our lazy president was also on vacation before this war even started. Bush spent a month at his ranch shortly before the September 11, 2001, attacks, when he could have been a bit more attentive to warning signs. When a president receives a briefing entitled "Bin Laden Determined to Strike Inside U.S." and tosses it aside to go chop down some trees, you have to wonder what Bush's thought process was. Isn't it strange how Bush was always caught napping when horrendous moments strike? You can see these chilling moments, frozen on the page through the magic of photography, throughout this book. Perhaps it's no coincidence that Bush was always slacking off when a disaster hit—because he was just slacking off all the time. Up here (tap temple with forefinger), Bush is *always* on vacation. Either that, or the idea of a terrorist attack early in his term that he could use for his war and civil-repression agenda sounded fine by him.

To be honest, Bush's work ethic did kick in for a period after 9/11. From the attacks until 2004, fueled by his unstoppable terror mandate, he ran all over the place dropping time bombs to explode, both domestic and foreign. By the time Hurricane Katrina hit in 2005, Bush was tired after all of his efforts and lazily dozed while the time bombs went off, one after the other. It seems like Bush viewed the presidency as the highest, cushiest spot on the employment ladder—the kind of job where you could take a nap whenever you wanted. Once he achieved the presidency and got a few wars started, it was O'Doul's time. He had already put in his work, struggling through classes at Yale and Harvard, bankrupting a few companies, eating hot dogs with the commoners at Texas Rangers Stadium, and throwing that switch on Ol' Sparky down at Texas State Prison. Once George finally got to be president, he must have said to his father, "All right, Poppy, I did it like you told me, the Bush family is controlling the country again! Can I go run around in the backyard now?"

It's obvious that Bush doesn't know how to do his day job, but he doesn't know how to take a vacation either. As U.S. General Philip Sheridan said in 1868, "If I owned Texas and Hell, I would rent Texas and live in Hell." Oh, but Bush's roots run deep in this blasted land. Most people normally go on vacation to places that are better than where they're stuck all the time—perhaps a balmy equatorial island paradise, scented with tropical flowers, where the turquoise ocean laps gently upon the soft white sand. In contrast to us normal people, Bush likes to escape to the dusty scrublands of central Texas, where it's so blazing hot that crickets roast on the ground when they stop jumping. One of Bush's favorite activities is betting on which aide or reporter will be the next to drop from heat exhaustion. While on vacation, Bush works hard to make this arid landscape even less appealing by chopping down and burning all the trees on his property. What

Marco Langari/AFP/Getty Images

Russia invades Georgia, after a Georgian attack on a breakaway
province the day before.

Larry Downing/Reuters

Official Bikini Inspector Bush tests the backbone of our
nation's female sand volleyball personnel.

a freak. Maybe the reason that Bush doesn't care about the environment is that the view from his back window looks like hell, and he can't imagine anyone wanting to preserve something like that.

Isn't it also a bit disturbing to consider that Bush's idea of a good time on vacation isn't meeting new people from interesting cultures, exploring historic and religious sites, or appreciating the beauty of nature across the planet, but rather ripping the shit out of something with a chainsaw? The stink of gasoline, the ear-splitting whine, the spray of stinging wood chips, in the heat of a 100-degree day—these are Bush's favorite things? While he's at his job, this must be what he dreams about doing. What issues is Bush working through here? When Bush was sitting through some long G8 speech

The Bush Workout

Physical fitness is very important to George W. Bush; it was a way to "clear his mind" of all those negative headlines about crashing stock markets and dead American soldiers. Here is Bush's typical workout, developed with his personal trainer, Jeff "Bulldog" Gannon.

Warm-up: Dodge reporters' questions at press conference	15 minutes practicing that judo choke hold he learned from Putin
Cardio: 30 minutes of chasing Secretary of State Condoleezza Rice around White House, trying to kiss her	Seated bouncing on large rubber exercise ball, for as long as it's entertaining
Weight-training: 2 sets of 10 biceps curls	5 more girly push-ups
15-minute break to admire flexed physique in full-length mirror	**Cooldown:** 10 minutes of Transcendental Meditation in full lotus position upon the meaning of the universe (optional)
10 girly push-ups	
25 deep lunges (useful training for kneeling before Cheney)	**Post-workout recovery shake:** 1 scoop whey protein powder, 2 cups skim milk, 8 crushed Xanax tablets, shot of Wild Turkey
5 minutes on mechanical rodeo bull to develop core strength	

in Europe, listening to some foreign leader drone on and on, did he fantasize about sawing through the man's face with his chainsaw? When Bush had to read the U.S. Constitution in a last-minute presidential GED course that he was required to take, he often thought to himself, "Jesus Christ, I wish I could just chainsaw this fucking thing instead of having to read it."

Although Bush has let himself go a bit over the last few years, he was an exercise fanatic for most of his presidency. Workouts were like mini-vacations for Bush, where he could clear his mind of all of those disastrophes and catasters and whatnot. Less than two months after 9/11, the *New York Times* reported that Bush had clocked his fastest time for a one-mile run in a decade. He was jogging four miles a day. It's heartwarming to know that while we were all afraid to go outside for fear of catching anthrax, Bush was out galloping in the sunshine. However, in the August 23, 2002, issue of *Runner's World* magazine, George confessed how hard it was for the leader of the free world to get in a brisk run. "I try to go for longer runs, but it's tough around here at the White House on the outdoor track. It's sad that I can't run longer. It's one of the saddest things about the presidency," said Bush. Take heart, George. We will rejoice with you when you strap on your shorts and a terry-cloth headband once again and go trotting off down the road. It's a beautiful new day indeed when the most dangerous weapon Bush can deploy is some Tough-Actin' Tinactin on his athlete's foot.

During his debate with President-to-Be Barack Obama, even twitchy, lurching, old John McCain said that the nation needed a "steady hand on the tiller." This statement could have reflected McCain's racist assumption that black men can't yacht, but it was also a veiled attack on George W. Bush.

If we need a steady hand on the tiller, whose hand has been on the tiller for the last eight years? Presumably Bush was passed out drunk on the top deck, getting a terrible, bright-red sunburn, with his bare foot caught in the captain's wheel, steering the U.S.S. *America* straight into the Bermuda Triangle.

Even Bush's professed Christianity is a sort of mental vacation for him. This world doesn't seem to matter too much to a true believer like Bush, who talks to God in top-secret, classified conversations on a regular basis. With his long-term goals of spreading "democracy" across the world, no matter how many people got squashed along the way, Bush seemed to be focused on the hereafter (although he may not like where he ends up). When a president believes in guardian angels, it can make them pretty lazy about protecting people. What about the hurricane victims, the stock market victims, the former-home-owner victims, the roadside-bomb-in-Iraq victims? Bush's answer always was, "Let God sort them out." His faith in laissez-faire Christianity is strong. If something blew up, Bush would just pray afterward to put everything in God's hands, and for Americans to find the strength to struggle through. We did the struggling, while he took a praycation. Back when Bush was governor in Texas, he proclaimed June 10, 2000, to be a statewide "Jesus Day," on which he urged "all Texans to answer the call to serve those in need." After all, the Bushes don't serve nobody. Let the peasants serve one another while the Bushes frolic at their luxurious century-old Kennebunkport oceanfront estate.

When Hurricane Katrina hit and the vacationing Bush dawdled in his response, rapper/producer Kanye West had something to say during a live telecast on MTV of a benefit

Tale of the Tape

How tight is this tag team?

Topic	Jesus Christ	George W. Bush
Faith	Invoked the will of God to spread peace and love	Invoked the will of God to spread war and torture
Economy	Chased money lenders out of the temple	Gave $700 billion to Wall Street with no oversight
Poverty	Created loaves and fishes for hungry masses	Cut spending on programs for hungry masses
Miracle	Raised Lazarus from the dead	Raised Cheney and Rumsfeld from the Nixon administration
Courage	Proclaimed, "All they that take the sword, shall perish by the sword"	Proclaimed to enemy soldiers, "Bring 'em on"
Magic	Turned water into wine	Turned wine into alcoholism
Hair	Was renowned for long, flowing, glossy hair	Unconditioned hair often looked dry and frizzy
Crime	Fraternized with criminals in an effort to redeem them	Employed criminals in an effort to enrich them
Defense	Told His followers to "turn the other cheek"	Told his followers to "launch the other cruise missile"
Downfall	Betrayed by His apostle, Judas Iscariot	Betrayed by White House press secretary Scott McClellan

concert for New Orleans. Going off-script, Kanye loudly proclaimed to America's viewing public that "George Bush doesn't care about black people." That's a completely true statement, Mr. Kan, the Louis Vuitton Don. I would expand that statement to say that Bush doesn't care about any kind of people, unless they're close family members (but not the Mexican ones); CEOs of oil, weapons, or financial corporations; or the King of Saudi Arabia. But let's not be too hard on George. Once again, our president gave us something to truly be thankful for—all those days that he spent on vacation. Imagine the damage he could have done if he was able to work seven days a week, 365 days a year. All of us—black and white, Republican and Democrat, male and female, young and old—would probably be out in the streets hunting squirrels for dinner tonight.

Our Global Torture Network

Zapping Terror in the Genitals

E ven though we've never been afraid to jump into combat, Americans have always prided themselves on their good sportsmanship in war. This is a relic of polite manners from World War II, when our enemies were the ones with the torture camps, while we handed out Hershey bars to the kids. We thought we were the side that treated our prisoners humanely, instead of sticking them in cages and stabbing bamboo shoots up under their toenails. We did bomb the Japanese and German civilian population without mercy, but at least we stopped killing them as soon as their fascist governments were overthrown. This stands in contrast to Nazi Germany and Imperial Japan, which continued to torture and kill people in lands they had conquered. We also interned many Japanese-Americans during the war in camps, but at least didn't turn them into lampshades and soap. And even though every U.S. war since WWII has featured more incalculable violence against civilians, we still like to think of ourselves as the square-jawed hero who bursts into the enemy prison to save the guy who's getting tortured—not the smirking villain hunched over his screaming hostage, wielding a scalpel and blowtorch.

That evil overlord has been running the country for the last eight years. To fulfill his lust for torture, Bush had to do away with laws that reflected our traditional revulsion.to it. How did Bush get his torture train rolling? Shortly after 9/11, White House legal counsel Alberto Gonzalez drafted a memo which stated that the international Geneva Conventions on the treatment of prisoners of war would not apply to anyone captured in the War on Terror. Picking up steam in February 2002, President Bush signed a secret order authorizing the CIA to set up covert prisons overseas, outside U.S. borders and our national law, to question prisoners with unprecedented torture techniques. Bush greased the tracks for torture by withdrawing the United States from the International Criminal Court on May 7, 2002. This granted immunity from the court for U.S. citizens suspected of torture, war crimes, and other atrocities. U.S. soldiers overseas are immune from prosecution, while politicians and CIA agents can claim diplomatic immunity (just like the villain in *Lethal Weapon 2*—Bush loved that guy).

There were grinding noises and shrieks of pain coming out of the darkness for two years. But on April 28, 2004, in a cloud of sulfurous stench, Bush's torture train burst out of the mouth of the tunnel to Hades into the bright light of day. Hundreds of photographs and videotapes were released from the U.S.-run Abu Ghraib prison in Iraq, depicting shocking abuse and torture of detainees by U.S. soldiers. Most of these

New CIA Torture Manual

Excerpts from the CIA's Counterintelligence Interrogation *manual, updated in 2005 to address the Abu Ghraib prison scandal, show that our torture professionals use only the most cutting-edge techniques to keep Americans safe.*

Section 3, page 21
"Interrogators must wash hands after smearing detainees with human excrement."

Section 2, page 15
"Detainees may not be left shackled in extreme stress positions (such as the Hanging Hogtie, the Reverse Lobster, the Shoulder-Popper, or the Salute to Ronald Reagan) for a period of longer than twelve hours, unless rejuvenated on an hourly basis with a vigorous slap across the face with a sixteen-inch length of garden hose, in which case detainees may be left in the aforementioned stress positions for a period of up to twenty-four hours."

Section 5, page 46
"Trained interrogation dogs may be denied food for a maximum of only eight hours before being employed in an interrogation session."

Section 7, page 54
"All sodomy on adult male detainees (aged 18–95) must be performed with the standard-issue AP-76 anal penetration device. The advanced carbon-fiber technology of this interrogation tool was developed at a cost of $10.5 million— be sure to read and follow all AP-76 safety instructions so as to not break the device. For juvenile male detainees, sodomy performed with a common household broomstick is permissible."

Section 2, page 29
"Waterboarding must be performed with ten gallons of clean tap water. If local indoor plumbing has not yet been provided by Halliburton, Inc. military contractors and tap water is not available, urine may be substituted."

Section 4, page 37
"Detainees must have all clothing removed and then be weighed before they are ordered to assume a human-pyramid formation. The heaviest detainees must be positioned in the pyramid's bottom row."

Section 8, page 65
"If detainee experiences a permanent cessation of life functions during an interrogation session, detainee remains must be cleaned, packed in ice, and sealed in a human-remains pouch (HRP) before transportation to Camp Liberty Mass Human Waste Disposal Site #23."

Section 1, page 1
"The possession or use of photographic and video-recording cameras by interrogators during interrogation sessions is strictly forbidden."

detainees had committed no crimes. They were picked off the street in huge arrest sweeps of Iraqi men in order to find information about insurgent attacks. Rush Limbaugh might want you to think that the Abu Ghraib torture was the equivalent of frat boys letting off some steam, but this is much more than noogies, Indian burns, or even atomic wedgies. This is jumping on someone's leg (already wounded by gunfire) with such force that it could not thereafter heal properly, then pounding on that leg with a metal baton. This is sodomizing prisoners, urinating on prisoners, and pouring phosphoric acid on them. This is anal rape with broomsticks and tying ropes to men's penises and dragging them across the floor. Just to be clear, this is beating, stressing, and torturing people until they die. It's all very difficult to deal with, but I'm sure that Mr. Limbaugh would want to get his facts straight on this subject.

Since when did the American fighting man start sodomizing the enemy? There is no record of colonial American patriots in the Revolutionary War buggering the bung-holes of the British Redcoats. U.S. soldiers were not tempted by the golden brown buttocks of the Mexican Army in 1846. Union and Confederate soldiers did not break ranks at Gettysburg in a mad charge to mount one another. The Civil War was brother against brother, not brother on brother. And the Marines did not raise the Stars and Stripes on Iwo Jima planted in a fallen Japanese soldier's rectum. Bush and Rumsfeld certainly did transform our nation's military, into a mobile, high-tech, twenty-first-century ass-raping machine.

You could go on for pages with all of the twisted sex games and malicious torture, but one technique demands mention. It is known as a Palestinian hanging (it's an Israeli term), but is in fact crucifixion. The hands are shackled behind the back, to a wall. Over time, the prisoner grows tired and slumps forward, constricting the lungs and causing asphyxiation. A tortuous death by crucifixion can take hours or even days. A CIA interrogator in Abu Ghraib killed Manadel al-Jamadi in 2003 using this torture technique. Unfortunately, Mr. al-Jamadi did not rise from the dead three days later.

There is no mention of any useful information extracted from the torture victims of Abu Ghraib. There was no clear goal, no organizing principle. The torture program seemed to serve no apparent purpose other than reveling in physical, psychological, and sexual sadism. If there is one lasting image of Bush's professed desire to bring freedom to the Middle East, let it be the famous freedom-loving dominatrix in combat boots, Pvt. Lynndie England, holding a dog leash attached to the neck of a grimacing, naked Iraqi man sprawled on the ground. Hundreds more photos and videos from Abu Ghraib, said to be "significantly worse" by a senator who was allowed to see them, were kept secret by the Pentagon. Bush claimed that the torture was the work of a few "bad apples" among his underlings and denied any knowledge or approval of torture by anyone in his administration.

"We do not torture."

—George W. Bush, November 7, 2005

Yet on October 15, 2008, it was revealed that in 2003 and 2004 Bush had issued two secret memos to the CIA specifically endorsing the agency's use of torture techniques. It was apparent for all to see that Bush had blatantly lied in 2005 when he said we don't torture. It was a lie that covered up the very serious crimes that Bush was authorizing, but his lie was blown wide open. No one really seemed to care that much. You know, McCain said something about Obama, and then Obama said something back, so we were busy with all that.

This lack of outrage regarding Bush's torture order brings up a troubling thought on the nature of human behavior. People don't like to be lied to, but they especially don't enjoy other people knowing that they were suckered. No one likes to bring up the fact that they got ripped off. As the subject of the lie becomes more serious, the more people want to avoid the shame and embarrassment of admitting that they were conned, to disastrous results. This is a grim observation if you consider the enormity of the lies and the depth of disaster that governments can create. Are we all so ashamed about U.S.-committed torture that we refuse to seek justice against its perpetrators? As Bush's lies have increased in scale, we have become more silent. Perhaps torture is not meant to get one person to talk, but rather to make everyone else shut up.

This scandal is about more than a few demented prison guards at Abu Ghraib. Bush's call to torture went out across a global network of secret torture camps. There is the notorious Camp Delta at the U.S. military base in Guantánamo Bay, Cuba, where torture started in 2001. Prisoners are being held and tortured on a fleet of U.S. Navy ships floating in the Indian Ocean. . . . It takes the brain a moment to fully comprehend the dark secrecy and utter lack of oversight that the words *torture ship* mean. Bush admitted in 2006 that the CIA operates a network of "black sites" around the world where "enhanced interrogation techniques" are used, which is a euphemism for jamming a fluorescent light tube up there, then breaking it. Who knows what fiendish tortures the CIA and military are still inflicting on helpless prisoners around the world?

Discovering useful information on possible future terrorism through the use of torture is as impossible as finding a WMD in a mountain of bullshit. And we're not even interrogating actual terrorists with PhDs from Terror University (wherever those guys are), but Afghan goatherds and random Iraqi dudes who are unfortunate enough to be between the ages of sixteen and sixty and who sleep in houses (U.S. Marines tend to break into those in the middle of the night to abduct terrorists to torture). Another reason why torture doesn't work is that insurgent fighters figured out a long time ago that it's best to operate in clandestine cells—a network of small groups not aware of each other's existence. Whether you're the French Resistance fighting the Nazis, the Algerian independence movement fighting the French, or the Iraqis fighting the Americans,

The Efficacy Of Torture

Torture is an exact science, with specific techniques that are used to extract certain types of information. Here are the most common techniques employed by the U.S. military's torture professionals, which were pulled out of somebody's ass with a pair of barbecue tongs.

Technique	Usefulness
Waterboarding	Threats against ports and waterways
Stress positions	Determining why the prisoner hates America so much
Attack dogs	Gaining information on collaborators/chewing off testicles
Sleep deprivation	Enhancing the prisoner's ability to hallucinate outlandish terror plots that will garner the interrogator a promotion
Sexual degradation	Getting lots of hits on YouTube
Forced sodomy	Unclear, but a great way for interrogators to blow off some steam

it's best to operate in this cell structure so your entire organization can't be rolled up in one stroke. That's a lot of fingernails you have to pull out before you can really get anywhere.

Along with his innovative torture techniques, Bush came up with the brilliant idea of paying money to informants in Iraq and Afghanistan who turn in alleged terrorists to the U.S. military. What a well-thought-out approach, perfectly suited to these two war-torn countries. Afghanistan's only industry is heroin, with a welter of violent, armed ethnicities and tribes vying for control of the black market. In Iraq, Sunnis and Shia still hate each other and are scrambling to either hold on to power or to seize power. In both countries, everyone is dirt poor and most people don't have a job, with unemployment as high as 70 percent. Sure, these are two situations where people will give you some rock solid leads on each other. Go ahead, offer these people a bounty payment to inform on each other as "terrorists." It's not like they would make false accusations against their rivals, or just turn in anybody to make a quick dinar.

Have you noticed how our growing comfort level with torture, perhaps influenced by the actions of our president, is reflected in the film and television entertainment that we are fed? There's always a movie or TV show on that features power drills being inserted into human bodies. It seems like a long time ago when we watched happy African-American families in brightly colored sweaters on prime time, learning, laughing, and loving in their tastefully decorated living rooms. Parents have very different viewing options these days. "Hey, kids, let's make a big bowl of popcorn, sit down together on the couch, and watch a young woman be manacled to a board, have steel clamps inserted into her mouth, a surgical incision made beneath her front lip, her front face pulled up to her eye-balls, and a forceps smashed through her nasal cavity into her brain, where her pituitary gland will be torn from her skull! But after the show ends, you kids have got to go straight to bed, okay?" Remember those saucy prostitutes on cop shows, whose function was to toss off a snappy one-liner to break the tension as they were led through bustling police stations? Now the cops spend all their time in the morgue, looking down in slow panning shots over the naked, bruised corpses of those prostitutes, trying to determine if they were raped before being dismembered, or vice versa.

To understand the closed loop of Bush's torture doc-trine, consider the case of Binyam Mohamed. He was seized in 2002 from Pakistan, then flown to a CIA prison in Morocco, where he was molested by proxy torturers. Yes, the CIA also has hulking, swarthy, foreign henchmen who do their bid-ding, as well as U.S. Army hillbilly grunts. The agents simply sit back during the grueling torture sessions and wait for the confession, not even getting their white gloves dirty. Binyam Mohamed couldn't take any more slashing of his genitals with a razor blade, so he told the CIA he was planning on setting off a radioactive dirty bomb in a major U.S. city. He is now awaiting trial for this imagined crime by a military tribunal in Guantánamo Bay. Torture leads to false confessions of failed terror threats, which are publicized as victories in the War on Terror, therefore increasing the prestige and budget of the War on Terror, which leads to more torture.

Could this be the real reason for torturing people—to extract false confessions of heinous terror plans, so that the men whose job it is to "fight terror" can continue to skim off over half of the United States Treasury every year? Do the leaders of the War on Terror use torture as a way to keep their numbers up, to make their terror-bust quotas every month, so that they can get a nice big boost to their paychecks and their departmental budgets? "See, this guy WAS a terrorist! Look at him still whining about it. Sure looks like that peace dividend of the post–Cold War era will have to go straight into the CIA black-ops budget after all. And go order some more cruise missiles, we're gonna need a lot of 'em for bombing that country this guy told us about." Are the latest attacks on Pakistan carried out with torture-guided missiles?

"This crusade, this war on terrorism is going to take a while."

—George W. Bush, September 16, 2001

Ah, the good old Crusades against the infidel Muslims. Bush also resurrected the Spanish Inquisition for us in his love for all things medieval. Besides Torquemada's major influence on Bush's personal philosophy, where does this eagerness to torture come from? Did George administer the most punishing swirlies in his Texas grade school? Did the death imagery that surrounded him in his secret Skull and Bones fraternity at Yale really get to him? Was seeing his first mock human sacrifice and immolation at the pagan Bohemian Grove ritual in Northern California a life-transforming event? Did Bush find executing retarded prisoners as the governor of Texas to be especially funny and entertaining? Or does Bush seek to inflict pain on others because he himself was molested by a senior family member with a Darth Vader's Torture Droid action figure as a tender young boy?

It is now clear that Bush's fraudulent WMD threats that led to the Iraq War and his phony terror alerts originated from torture sessions. Ibn al-Shaykh al-Libbi was waterboarded and given hypothermia treatment (stuck in a freezing meat locker wearing only a wet pair of boxer shorts?) until he coughed up a story about al-Qaeda's links to Saddam's WMD. When he later retracted this claim, ABC News found that al-Libbi had no knowledge of such weapons and had fabricated his statements because he was terrified of more harsh treatment. Bush waved this torture confession, from a man who was freezing to death, as more proof for us to invade Iraq. Another tortured prisoner who felt the excruciating pain of freedom was Abu Zubaydah. He was waterboarded, beaten, subjected to mock executions, and blasted with continuous deafening noise and bright lights for months. Bush squeezed from Zubaydah dozens of warnings of attacks—such as bombs in malls, banks, supermarkets, nuclear plants, apartment buildings, and public water systems—across the United States. Many of Bush's national terror threat alerts came from Zubaydah's pain-wracked hallucinations.

What would you confess to if someone had a pistol pointed to your head and they started counting down from five? Bush tortured his victims to get them to say what he wanted to hear them say. This illegal occupant of the White House essentially replaced the entire governmental system of the United States with a new, alien mechanism. Confessions were extracted through torture, outside of the United States and without any oversight of our Congress. That false, torture-produced information was then used to bully Congress into supporting Bush's declarations of war as well as the USA PATRIOT Act and the creation of the Department of Homeland Security.

This revolting system that Bush has trapped us in is a downward spiral of torture leading to war leading to more torture.

So the big question is, will this war criminal get away with it all? In his last few months in office, Bush, of course, worked hard to ensure that. He did his best to immunize himself from war crimes. Hundreds of hours of video was shot of Abu Zubaydah's torture sessions. These tapes could have definitively proven if Bush committed war crimes, but the tapes were destroyed. We know that four senior aides of Bush and Cheney—including, for example, David Addington, the chief legal architect of Bush's torture policies—discussed destroying the tapes. Bush also tried to ram a bill through Congress, without lubrication, that would redefine the treatment of detainees. Buried in this legislation is a provision that will pardon Bush and all members of his administration of any possible crimes connected with their torture of detainees. Under the War Crimes Act, violations of the Geneva Conventions are felonies—in some cases, punishable by death. When the U.S. Supreme Court ruled in 2006 that the Geneva Conventions applied to al-Qaeda and Taliban detainees, Bush started feeling the pressure. In an effort to avoid any possible prosecution, he did his best to get his bill signed into law.

Just in case destroying incriminating evidence and pardoning himself doesn't do the trick, Bush in 2006 allegedly bought 98,840 acres of land in Paraguay. Is this Bush's possible escape route, the classic South American getaway for right-wing fascists to avoid international justice? In early 2005, Paraguay passed a law that granted diplomatic immunity to U.S. military, such as our commander-in-chief, from the International Criminal Court if indicted for war crimes. If Bush is nowhere to be found after January 20, 2009, he's probably fleeing to Paraguay, hidden inside a shipping crate aboard a tramp steamer.

Perhaps Bush's torture scandal is not so un-American after all. Take a look at the men whom the CIA has always liked the best—the guys they pick to run foreign countries, after the CIA assassinates their democratically elected leaders: Saddam Hussein in Iraq, Pinochet in Chile, the Shah of Iran, General Suharto in Indonesia, Mobutu Sese Seko in Zaire, Batista in Cuba, Noriega in Panama. The list could go on. Every last goddamned one of them enjoyed viciously inflicting pain on helpless victims. This kind of leadership personality is what the CIA was drawn to. Are you really surprised that the CIA has something in common with sadistic third-world fascist torturers? George W. Bush has almost done us a favor with his torture scandal. Along with his blundering eagerness to torture, he was careless in making a paper trail that led back to him. Or maybe Bush just assumed that torture wasn't all that bad, and no one would be too upset about it. Well, are you? We might have to even give George a sincere thank-you for giving Americans the chance to honestly think about how we treat everybody else on this planet. With his failed cover-up of what America has been doing since the beginning of the Cold War, Bush has forced us to take a necessary and hard look at who we really are, and what we really stand for.

PATRIOT ACT POLICE STATE

Are You a Security Risk?

I s this how you spell *al-Qaeda*? Or is it *Al-Qaeda, al-Qaida,* or *al-Qa'ida*? Capitalization on the *al,* hyphen or no hyphen, and what's up with the apostrophe? There was even an *al-Kaeda* floating around for a while back there. For a copy editor, it's difficult to pin down, much like the real al-Qaeda. But over here on our side, the language is loud and clear. We have the USA PATRIOT Act, and those letters are in capitals for a reason. The name is an acronym, which stands for **U**niting and **S**trengthening **A**merica by **P**roviding **A**ppropriate **T**ools **R**equired to **I**ntercept and **O**bstruct **T**errorism. This body of law, passed in haste after the 9/11 attacks, was originally intended to be named the USA LICK THE BOOT OF FASCISM Act; but was renamed once George W. Bush ran out of ideas after **U**niting and **S**trengthening **A**merica by **L**iquidating and **I**nterrogating the **C**razy **K**illers That . . . Hate . . . Everything?

You have to admit, that acronym is pretty awesome, especially if you're a twelve-year-old boy with a crush on Ann Coulter. It's almost as good as when they told us that they were going to build the new Freedom Tower (again, a totally awesome stroke of make-believe) on the ashes of Ground Zero to a height of exactly 1,776 feet (my pet eagle, Ashcroft, just shed a glistening tear of pride). Yes, grown-ups actually came up with all of this. The PATRIOT Act would be even funnier if it hadn't given to a guy like George W. Bush the right to spy on, imprison, and abuse Americans. That's the part where the laughter dwindles.

Opposed by only one senator, the Honorable Russell Feingold of the great state of Wisconsin, the PATRIOT Act flew through a cringing Congress and was signed into law by Bush on October 26, 2001. It makes you wonder how Bush and his cronies even got the massive 342-page thing conceptualized in that time, let alone written, rammed through Congress, and signed in six weeks. Of course, the PATRIOT Act was already on the shelf, ready to go. Bush, Ashcroft, and the rest of the neoconservative core had been working on their wish list of civil liberties to revoke for a long time. No terrorist attack, no matter how horrendous, can ever cause a loss of the fundamental rights to American citizens guaranteed by our Constitution. Only the U.S. government, led by George W. Bush, can take away rights from Americans, and they've done quite a job of it so far.

It would have been nice if the Democrats who have been controlling Congress since 2006 had blown out the lit match that Bush always waved under our Constitution, but at least we had the librarians. They announced that they would start shredding the library-lending records of their patrons when the Department of Homeland Security announced its intention of snooping through our reading lists, presumably to find bookworms who were researching how to blow up a nuclear reactor at their local branch. Can you really find that at the library? Is that stuff over by the little fantasy castle in the kid's playtime reading circle, or next to the Danielle Steele

Antiterror Tactics

What measures did President Bush enact to fight terrorism in the homeland, and how effective have they been?

Tactics	Effectiveness
Color-coded threat advisory system	Publicly informing terrorists when our defenses are most relaxed
Removal of shoes at airports	Letting the terrorists know they'd better find a different article of clothing to hide their bombs in
"Free speech zone" cages for protestors at political conventions	Delegates not being terrorized by women with noticeable body hair
Random searches of citizens' bags at subway stations	Forcing the terrorists to walk two whole avenues to a subway station where the police are not searching bags
Wiretapping Americans' telephones	Ability to listen in on some pretty hot phone-sex calls
Federal access to citizens' library records	Marking any readers who are not a member of Oprah's Book Club as suspicious
Ability to search homes without the owners' knowledge	Homeland Security officers' ability to take anything from homes they might find useful to fight terror, or just some DVDs they haven't seen yet
Secret No Fly Lists for suspicious persons	Stopping journalists, academics, and antiwar activists from traveling to conventions where they might criticize the War on Terror

novels? It's fitting that the guardians of the nation's accumulated knowledge would be the ones to stand up to a dolt like Bush. Also, librarians are notorious hard-asses. Keeping a bunch of rowdy teenagers quiet is a lot tougher than attending $500-a-plate Democratic fund-raising dinners.

"If this were a dictatorship, it'd be a heck of a lot easier, heh heh heh. Just so long as I'm the dictator."
—George W. Bush, Washington, D.C., December 19, 2000

The PATRIOT Act was a big bucket of grease that Bush poured out on the slippery slope that leads down to tyranny. But you can't expect men like Bush to be happy with just one gift of increased power. They want it all. For example, the PATRIOT Act increased the ability of law enforcement agencies to search through American's telephone and e-mail communications, yet this wasn't enough for Bush. He had to secretly authorize the National Security Agency to wiretap, without a warrant, the phones of anyone he considered a threat. This deserves a closer look, at least for those who don't enjoy the bristly sound of a cop's mustache on the line while they're talking to their girlfriend on the phone.

The Foreign Intelligence Surveillance Act (FISA) Court was created after Nixon's phone-tapping abuses to prevent the president from spying on Americans without the approval of another branch of our government. You know, those good old checks and balances. FISA once made it necessary for the president to at least supply a warrant for tapping someone's phone, backed by a showing of probable cause, if he wanted to violate the Fourth Amendment of our Bill of Rights.

Probable cause is the lowest standard of proof in criminal law, and means "sufficient evidence to cause a reasonable person to believe that a crime may have been committed or is being committed." Bush did not want to be held even to this loose standard, and authorized wiretapping without FISA approval. By definition, if the president does not have probable cause for a warrant, it means that there is "insufficient evidence to cause a reasonable person to believe that a crime may have been committed or is being committed." President Bush circumvented the FISA Court—a court that has granted more than 99 percent of all the warrant applications it has ever received—because Bush wanted to wiretap Americans under circumstances in which no reasonable person could believe that the targeted American was engaged in criminal conduct of any kind (*analysis by attorney Seth Abramson*).

Bush's illegal wiretapping set a precedent in which the potential for abuse is simply too great. Our Founding Fathers gave us our Bill of Rights to protect us against governmental tyranny, such as guarding us against unreasonable searches and seizures in the privacy of our own homes and communications. The price of liberty is vigilance, and protecting our Bill of Rights as citizens is the only way to avoid our country ending up like East Germany. Of course, many Americans after the shock of 9/11 wanted the government to crack down on terrorists. Many supported the idea of giving the power to spy on and imprison people indefinitely without charges to a man like George W. Bush. In hindsight, we can all agree on what a disastrous move that was.

How would you like it if the FBI was wiretapping your phone and bugging your house? What if federal agents had broken into your home when you were not there, several times, to rifle through your papers and possessions? Imagine then being seized at your office by federal agents, handcuffed, hustled out into a waiting car, and thrown into prison with no charges filed against you. You would sit in that cell for weeks, with no explanation as to why you were being held. Your wife and children wouldn't even know where you were locked up, much less why. This is what really happened on May 6, 2004, to U.S. citizen Brandon Mayfield, an attorney in Portland, Oregon. The FBI claimed that they had Mayfield's fingerprints on a bag of detonators found at the scene of the train bombings in Madrid. They were completely wrong, and Mayfield was a completely innocent man. If Bush had his way, he might have been happy to imprison the entire state of Oregon indefinitely, on the charge of being a bunch of goddamn hippies.

"There ought to be limits to freedom."

—George W. Bush, May 21, 1999

Illegal searches and seizures lead to illegal arrests. This is where Bush's patriotic police state becomes very frightening. Are you ready for the 3 am knock on your door? After all, the terrorists could be anyone—what a convenient enemy for those who seek to consolidate their power and repress dissent. Everyone is a suspect, especially immigrants. Theoretically, that would make all of us a target for illegal incarceration, except for the Native Americans, who are already stuck in reservations. The PATRIOT Act allows for the indefinite imprisonment of any immigrant noncitizen whom the attorney general believes may cause a terrorist act—locking up people on no charges, for as long as the government wants, you know, Taliban-style justice. The British took away the power to imprison people without charges from their kings in the year 1305, but Bush wanted that power back.

In the days after the 9/11 attacks, 1,200 Middle Eastern and South Asian immigrants nationwide were swept up by the Immigration and Naturalization Service, now folded into the Homeland Security Department. At least 84 of these detainees were imprisoned at the Metropolitan Detention Center in Brooklyn, New York, and were detained under a "hold until cleared" policy. This policy permitted Muslim, Arab, or Pakistani noncitizens (whoops, and a few Indian Hindus who got caught up in the dragnet) to be imprisoned until cleared by the FBI, over eight months later. You can see where this is going. These men, who were imprisoned on no charges and eventually released with no charges, were subjected to an eight-month-long nightmare of severe physical and sexual abuse, humiliation, endless strip searches, sleep deprivation, solitary confinement, rotten food, exposure to freezing weather in light clothing, and yes, once again, having objects forcibly inserted into their rectums. I don't intend to always bring this up, it's the U.S. law enforcement officers and military personnel under the command of President Bush who insist on always returning to the uninvited anal penetration.

These men were typical, hardworking immigrants who came to America for a chance at a better life, but they were ambushed and imprisoned. These men were providing for their families, who were left without any means of financial support or any information on their missing husbands and fathers for eight months. You don't bounce back from eight months of torture, solitary confinement, and subhuman conditions. These innocent men, who had committed no crimes, are now scarred for life. Thanks to George W. Bush, we are all scarred, too. This wasn't Abu Ghraib in Iraq or Guantánamo Bay in Cuba. This prison is in the heart of Brooklyn, about a fifteen-minute walk from where I live. The Pakistani guy who I buy apples from at his fruit stand and the Arab guy who works at the corner deli are the same kind of guys who got smashed headfirst into concrete walls at the prison in our neighborhood.

"Our enemies are innovative and resourceful, and so are we. They never stop thinking about new ways to harm our country and our people, and neither do we."

—George W. Bush, Washington, D.C., August 5, 2004

Of course, you didn't have to be a Middle Eastern or Pakistani man to be persecuted in Bush's America. Criticism or dissent against Bush's policies has become increasingly criminalized. This goes far beyond the speeches where Bush stated that you either stand with us or against us; or that criticizing the president during a time of war (which he created) gives aid to the enemy. Domestic political groups with progressive agendas have been increasingly harassed, as undercover policemen using aliases have infiltrated organizational meetings, rallies, and group e-mail lists. The Maryland State Police classified fifty-three nonviolent antiwar and anti-death-penalty activists as terrorists from 2005 to 2006 and entered their names and personal information into state and federal databases that track terrorism suspects. The state police superintendent who authorized the operation defended the program, calling the activists "fringe people." Where exactly does this fringe begin? These Americans who peacefully opposed war and executions were labeled with computerized crime tags such as "terrorism—anti-government" and "terrorism—antiwar protesters." Welcome to Bush's bizarro-America, where those who speak peacefully against murder are labeled as crazed murderers.

There are now more than one million Americans on the No Fly List, who are not allowed to travel on airplanes because of their political views, because they have the same name as a suspicious person, or for no logical reason at all. The right to travel freely is a cornerstone of countries with basic human rights. One American citizen on the No Fly List is Sam Adams (yes, that's his real name), who you think would come across as a patriotic guy. Sam Adams has to struggle through endless obstacles if he tries to get onto a plane, or, for the time being, have his parents do the struggling for him. Suspected terrorist Sam Adams is five years old.

Fly List

Who are the more than 1 million people who have lost their right to travel freely under the USA PATRIOT Act?

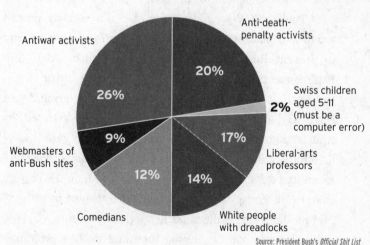

- Antiwar activists — 26%
- Anti-death-penalty activists — 20%
- Swiss children aged 5-11 (must be a computer error) — 2%
- Liberal-arts professors — 17%
- White people with dreadlocks — 14%
- Comedians — 12%
- Webmasters of anti-Bush sites — 9%

Source: President Bush's *Official Shit List*

113

In 2002, Minnesota expanded its legal definition of terrorism to include actions "intended to interfere with the conduct of government or the right of lawful assembly." This precedent led to the chilling police state on display at the Republican National Convention in Saint Paul in early September 2008. Hordes of paramilitary riot police in their ridiculous black stormtrooper armor and gas masks, brandishing shotguns loaded with you-don't-want-to-find-out, filled the streets of Saint Paul. They used pepper spray, teargas, flash grenades, and batons on peaceful protestors. If Bush had actually been invited to his own party's convention, they probably would have rolled out the tanks and flamethrowers. Credentialed, independent journalists who attempted to simply document this Orwellian scene—including Amy Goodman and her crew from Pacifica Radio's *Democracy Now!* program—were thrown to the ground, handcuffed, and arrested for no reason. Meanwhile, the mainstream media focused on the important issues, like Sarah Palin describing herself as a vicious attack dog wearing lipstick.

The RNC Welcoming Committee was a feisty protest group that planned to carry out direct actions in an attempt to prevent Republican delegates from entering the Saint Paul convention center, including devastating terror strategies such as the old spreading-marbles-on-the-ground gag. Eight leaders of this group were preemptively arrested, by squads of police breaking into their homes with guns drawn, before the group had even committed any actions. They face *seven and a half years* in prison if convicted, on the illusory charges of "conspiracy to riot in furtherance of terrorism." And we thought that the 2004 Republican convention in New York City was bad, when one thousand people, protestors and bystanders alike, were swept off the street and held for twenty-four to forty-eight hours, bound at the wrists inside razor-wire-topped chain-link cages, inside a huge, filthy, diesel-oil-and-asbestos–ridden, concrete-floored warehouse on Pier 57, dubbed "Guantánamo-on-the-Hudson." It all makes one wonder what would happen if you had marched in *support* of Bush's bloodshed, holding signs like "Kill More Terrorists," "More Blood for Oil," and "Crusaders, RISE Against the Muslims!"? Would you get fired upon with rubber bullets, pepper sprayed, beaten, and hauled away by riot police? Or would the cops just give you a benevolent smile and ask you kindly to not block traffic, please?

The threat of the police state isn't aimed solely at immigrant workers, scruffy protestors in Saint Paul, journalists from public radio, or teenagers trying to go to a movie in Manhattan when the Republican convention happens to be in town. *Police state* is too mild a term—what Bush really wanted was our nation under martial law. The Defense Authorization Act of 2007 (H.R. 5122), which was signed into law by Bush on October 17, 2006, in a private Oval Office ceremony, allows the president to declare a "public emergency" and station U.S. military troops anywhere in the country in order to "suppress public disorder." Yes, this country once had laws that prohibited the use of the national military by the president against American civilians, before Bush erased them. Those laws were passed in 1807. The United States of America held together fine for over two hundred years, making it through our Civil War, Nazi Germany and Imperial Japan, and the Soviet Union without resorting to the threat of martial law, but apparently a few hundred bearded guerrillas in Afghanistan is all it took to make Bush whip out his golden martial-law pen, embossed with his own name, that he's been waiting to use all this time.

This isn't a toothless piece of legislation. According to the *Army Times* on September 30, 2008, the 3rd Infantry Division's 1st Brigade of the U.S. Army has been already deployed for full duty inside the United States, another first for Bush. Our new Homeland Attack Force is just back from spending thirty-five of the last sixty months in "full battle rattle" patrolling Iraq. Reading stories from Iraq—such as the one about a gunner opening fire on an Iraqi crowd with a .50-caliber mounted machine gun after a rubber flip-flop sandal was thrown at his U.S. tank—have suddenly become much more relevant. As reported in the *Army Times,* this hardened battle force is expected to help with domestic "civil unrest and crowd control" and is equipped with "the first ever nonlethal package that the army has fielded," referring to "nonlethal weapons designed to subdue unruly or dangerous individuals without killing them." Gee, thanks. Did you see that episode of *Jackass* where Johnny Knoxville gets a beanbag bullet shot into his abdomen, which is what this army brigade is toting? *Subdue* isn't the word, it's more like *brutally wounding someone badly enough to leave their entire torso bruised for months.*

To get these troops into the spirit of "nonlethal" weaponry, the soldiers have been Tasering each other. "I was the first guy in the brigade to get Tasered," said one soldier quoted in the *Army Times,* describing the experience as "your worst muscle cramp ever—times ten throughout your whole body. I'm not a small guy, I weigh two hundred and thirty pounds . . . it put me on my knees in seconds." Once the 1st Brigade completes its one-year deployment, "expectations are that another, as yet unnamed, active-duty brigade will take over and that the mission will be a permanent one." Could you please get some change going, and change the law back to when the president couldn't use the army on civilians, Mr. New President from on High, the Most Glorious Barack Hussein Obama the First?

The spiked club of martial law has been waved by Bush over even the United States Congress. This isn't "unfounded conspiracy theory" concerning martial law (which, you have to admit, was totally right on this stuff); you can watch a congressman say it on C-SPAN. Our elected representatives were threatened with martial law in early October 2008, if the "emergency" $700 billion bailout bill was not quickly passed to address the financial crisis. *Martial law* means that the separation of powers which our Founding Fathers exalted in our Constitution are gone, and only the all-powerful executive branch rules.

Representative Brad Sherman of California's 27th congressional district told the House that he personally knew of several congressional representatives who said they were threatened with martial law if they voted against the bailout. "The only way they can pass this bill is by creating and sustaining a panic atmosphere. That atmosphere is not justified," Sherman stated. "Many of us were told in private conversations that if we voted against this bill on Monday that the sky would fall, the market would drop two or three thousand points the first day, another couple of thousand the second day, and a few members were even told that there would be martial law in America if we voted no." So that's why Bush gave huge government contracts to Kellogg Brown & Root, a division of Cheney's Halliburton, to build large-scale detention camps at undisclosed locations inside the United States to hold tens of thousands of "fringe people" who might need to be "subdued." How different is the threat of martial law compared to the real thing? If a 400-pound brute walks up to you and threatens to punch you in the mouth unless you give him all your money, the end result is the same as if he had actually smashed your teeth out and grabbed the money out of your pocket. You're still out 700 billion bucks.

But hey, this is what we have to deal with in the Age of Terror, right? We want increased security to keep us safe, and happily accept a little pepper gas here, a little foreign object inserted into the the rectum there, maybe certain swaths of the population in concentration camps for our own protection, if we all get extra-naughty. We enjoy the sight of paramilitary troops with helmets and machine guns on our street corners, and don't mind at all if federal agents break into our homes to seize our personal literature, books, computers, and digital files to search for any stain of terrorism. Thank you again, George W. Bush, for protecting us! We think the idea of the police having a truck-mounted "heat ray" microwave gun that can scorch whole crowds of people, sending them fleeing with pain, is exactly the thing we need to keep us safe. I mean, the terrorists could be anywhere! What if they all decided to jump out at the same time and suddenly combined into an unstoppable terror mob? We could use that heat ray for sure!

And how is the War on Terror going again? Is victory in sight? Besides the chaos, waste, and demented carnage of our foreign wars, that is. Are we at least capturing terrorists and chasing down the al-Qaeda killers who plot the destruction of our homeland? Have we caught the people behind 9/11, the crime that started this war? Only forty-eight hours after the 9/11 attacks, the FBI released the names and photos of the nineteen hijackers claimed to be on the planes. Eight of those "hijackers" stepped forward to publicly say that those names and photos belonged to them, and that they were clearly alive, and not kamikaze terrorists. The FBI still hasn't revised their original list. A year after the 9/11 attacks, FBI chief Robert Mueller admitted to CNN twice that "there is no legal proof to prove the identities of the suicidal hijackers." So the FBI doesn't have definitive names and photos of the people who actually hijacked those planes on 9/11 quite yet, but they're going to keep working extra-hard on that, totally. Oh, and the Freedom Tower will be completed at Ground Zero this year.

But Osama bin Laden was the guy behind 9/11, of course. He's the real target for an intelligent pursuit of the War on Terror, right, Barack? It's puzzling as to why there is no mention of 9/11 on the FBI's Ten Most Wanted list for Osama, then. The chief of Investigative Publicity for the FBI, Rex Tomb, explains this simply: "The reason why 9/11 is not mentioned on Osama bin Laden's Most Wanted page is because the FBI has no hard evidence connecting bin Laden to 9/11." The only crimes that are on bin Laden's Most Wanted page are for the bombings at the U.S. embassies in Tanzania and Kenya in 1998, which killed roughly two hundred people. Presumably Barack Obama could pursue bin Laden for the crime of attacking his father's homeland of Kenya. At least that mad campaign would be based in fact, unlike George W. Bush's assertion that bin Laden was the mastermind of 9/11.

So there hasn't been much effort to figure out the crime that actually started this Reign of Terror, but the Department of Homeland Security has done their desperate best to scrape up some phony terror plots to keep the whole narrative (and their budget) going. "These Middle Eastern terrorists were videotaping at Disney World while plotting a terror attack!" No, they were Middle Eastern tourists who were videotaping at Disney World, because that's what you do at Disney World. Besides, that Epcot Center is indestructible. It's, like, from space.

Catching the true perpetrators of 9/11 doesn't seem to matter to Bush, but there's plenty of time and effort to spend on scraping up some broke and unemployed patsies, entrapping them with offers of money, then trotting them out as a diabolical threat to the nation. The most laughable yet frightening (those two qualities were like peanut butter and jelly with Bush) domestic hoax of the War on Terror is the case in 2006 of the Liberty City Seven—seven young Haitian and African-American men from the impoverished Liberty City area of Miami, one of the poorest neighborhoods in the country. They are all unemployed or semiemployed, and several are homeless. They were offered $50,000 by an undercover FBI informant to spend on equipment if they swore an oath to al-Qaeda. These down-on-their-luck brothers tried to take the money and run, when they got busted. The funny part was when Attorney General Alberto Gonzales croaked "these men were prepared to wage a full ground war against the U.S.," and it was obvious to everyone else that these dudes intended to spend about $49,975 of that al-Qaeda money on weed. When they were arrested at their abandoned warehouse (by a paramilitary police strike force, as shown on television), their arsenal for full-on war consisted of some army boots and one registered handgun. I happen to have an old samurai sword and a comfortable pair of sneakers in my apartment, but I don't think I'm prepared for a full ground war against the armed forces of the United States.

The frightening part about the Liberty City Seven is that Bush tried to expand the War on Terror to the ghettos of America. Instead of an Arab or Pakistani face, he tried to put an African-American face onto the shapeless threat of terrorism. It was an attempt at a great leap forward for Bush's enemies list, at the expense of the people who have suffered the most from state-sponsored terror in the course of our nation's history. Do you see how the label of "terrorist" floats so freely at the command of Bush? First it was bin Laden, then it drifted to the Taliban, then it came down on some falafel-cart guys over here, then it sailed over to Saddam Hussein but not the people of Iraq, and then it *did* include many people in Iraq, then it sticks to attorneys in Oregon, protestors in Minnesota, and black men in Miami. The defendants in the Liberty City Seven case were found "not guilty" on their charges of terrorism, but the U.S. government intends to bring the case back to trial in a second attempt to justify the continued existence of their bogus War on Terror.

That's what Bush always told us. We're at war. All of us here at home have to make some sacrifices, give up our civil liberties, just let those constitutional rights that have protected us against state tyranny for centuries dissolve, so that our brave commanders can more easily capture the terrorists who threaten us all. Wait a minute—they're not capturing terrorists, but allowing them to escape? Well, that is a deal-breaker right there, George. Osama bin Laden and his cohorts escaped again and again, and not only from Tora Bora in Afghanistan, when the United States covered only three of the four possible escape routes. "Shucks, they snuck out the back door! Sorry." Bush gave billions of dollars to Pakistan's military, but I guess that wasn't enough to block a mountain pass for us. Before the standoff, or rather, the slink-off at Tora Bora, Osama bin Laden and his entourage were cruising around Afghanistan in highly visible convoys of hundreds of trucks and vehicles. As the war "drew to a close" in November of 2001, the elite of al-Qaeda, approximately a thousand fighters, were flown in an orderly airlift from the northern Afghan city of Kunduz to Pakistan, aboard a half-dozen Pakistani Air Force cargo planes. Don't take my word for it, take Pulitzer Prize–winning journalist Seymour Hersh's.

So there you have it—Bush gave $5 billion of our money in military aid to Pakistan, who used that money to fly al-Qaeda members to safety. There is no way that the United States did not know about these al-Qaeda escape flights to Pakistan. In November of 2001, the airspace of Afghanistan was the most closely watched airspace on the planet. Our satellites and surveillance planes have the capability to zoom in on a pile of goat dung in Afghanistan and determine what the goat ate for lunch. And now our new President Obama wants to take the fight further into Pakistan, where bin Laden and all his bad guys are, thanks to Bush. Perfect. This movie always needs its master villain; otherwise the movie is over if the villain is captured or killed. There is no ending to this epic terror drama, we're all just stuck in this dark theater of pain that Bush has created for us. Hey, why is the floor of this movie theater so sticky? Oh, we're sitting in several inches of coagulated blood.

"Can we win? I don't think you can win it."

—George W. Bush, responding to the question of whether the War on Terror was winnable, *Today* show interview, August 30, 2004

There's a reason why they tell us that this war will go on forever. It's going to take a while to get Americans warmed up to the idea of the government wiretapping their phones, imprisoning people indefinitely on no charges, and deploying the military against unarmed civilians. As one after another civil liberty of ours fades away, it brings to mind the old wives' tale of putting a frog in hot water. If you drop a frog straight into boiling water, it will jump out. But if you put the frog into a pot of cool water, and only gradually heat up the water, little by little, the frog will accept each incremental temperature change. Slowly, eventually, over time, that water is boiling and that frog is cooked. The domestic martial law police state isn't designed to capture the terrorists. It's designed for us.

Our Sagging Infrastructure

What Will Collapse Next?

Hurricane Katrina was the moment when everyone realized that we weren't in Kansas anymore. The guy who was supposed to be driving the car wasn't at the wheel, the car had fallen into the lake, and Bush had locked all of the doors. All we could do was watch the water rising through the windows. Many of us had feasted on the red, raw meat of Afghanistan and Iraq that Bush had thrown our way, and at least Bush seemed like the man in charge, even if he was charging us straightforward into the enemy guns. But when the hurricane hit, everyone finally saw clearly who George W. Bush was: an oblivious patrician who delivered a birthday cake to John McCain in Arizona and doodled on a guitar at another photo-op while a major American city, with some of the most unique and valuable contributions to our national culture, thrashed to stay alive in the rising waters.

"I don't think anybody anticipated the breach of the levees."

—George W. Bush, September 1, 2005, two days after receiving warnings from experts that Hurricane Katrina would breach New Orleans' levees

Bush's constant message, ever since 9/11, was that he was the one who would keep us safe. He was the tough cowboy who would stay up all night on his horse while we slept around the campfire, keeping his squinty eyes peeled for any approaching threats. However, we should have remembered Bush's reverse-speak speech disorder. When he said the words "I will keep you safe," what he actually meant was, "I will leave thousands of you stranded on rooftops in your flooded city for days, without food, water, medicine, security, or help of any kind, while I wrap up my month-long vacation." When Bush told us he would provide "steady leadership in a time of change," he actually meant "I'll appoint an old friend's college buddy to run the Federal Emergency Management Agency, whose previous job was running horse shows for the International Arabian Horse Association, from which he was fired." When Bush said that he was a "compassionate conservative," he actually meant "I will cram thirty thousand of you into the Superdome for a week, with no air-conditioning, running water, garbage disposal, or toilets, then send my mom out to say how all of you poor black people are really enjoying your free stay at the stadium."

Hurricane Katrina transformed all of Bush's photo ops of him hugging African-American children from ridiculous to grotesque. The goal of getting black people to vote Republican is about as realistic as killing every single terrorist in the whole world, but Bush was a dreamer. He was fine with having a black kid sit on his lap in an effort to scrape up a few votes,

President Bush's Greatest Moments—August 29, 2005

Bush and McCain didn't even bother to eat a piece.

These folks could really go for a piece of cake right about now.

but when it came time to rescue those kids from the roof of a submerged house, he wasn't so into it.

Found floating face-down in the floodwaters of New Orleans were 1,836 bloated bodies. Body counts were usually a political boost for Bush throughout his presidency, whether they tallied Taliban fighters or New Yorkers, but the death toll in New Orleans hurt him. While the death toll of the 9/11 attacks rallied our terrified nation to support Bush, the dead of New Orleans stripped away his illusion that he could protect us from harm. Katrina, of course, was a natural disaster—no one can stop a hurricane. But we expect our government to prepare for inevitable natural disasters and to help us after the storm has passed. That's what governments are for: to project organized human power to deal with problems that are too large for individual citizens to handle.

Instead of providing that help, Bush gave us his concerned flyover of New Orleans after Katrina aboard *Air Force One*. The starving, sick, newly homeless population of New Orleans looked up from their drowned city, wiping raw sewage from their eyes, to joyfully see that gloriously tiny white speck high in the sky. Warmed by Bush's concern beaming down upon them from 10,000 feet, the survivors burst into a spontaneous cheer of "Four More Years! Four More Years! Four More Years!" At least that's how our president's mother imagined it: ". . . they felt like when he flew over, that it made all the difference in their lives," said Barbara Bush to Larry King on CNN. It really was touching to watch these circling vultures tell each other how great they were while thirty thousand terrified people huddled inside the nightmarish Superdome. We will never forget Bush's immortal compliment to Michael Brown, the fired horse-judge turned FEMA chief who sent out e-mails such as "Can I quit now?" during the disaster: "Brownie, you're doing a heck of a job." Sweet little Brownie's soft cheeks creased into a smile as he closed his eyes and meekly lowered his head, accepting Bush's tender compliment like it was the soft touch of an angel's wings.

All the cute nicknames and pats on the back were a lame cover-up for how Bush's preexisting policies magnified the tragedy of Katrina. New Orleans and the Gulf Coast, obviously vulnerable to catastrophic storms, were left even more vulnerable in 2005, thanks to Bush. He had cut funding for the Army Corps of Engineers' proposed repair of hundreds of miles of levees in the region. After 9/11, Bush folded FEMA into the conglomeration of twenty-two agencies known as the shiny new Department of Homeland Security, which preferred to run around playing Gestapo instead of thinking about actual homeland security. Bush slashed FEMA's budget and installed hacks from his political campaigns into the demoralized agency's top positions. These appointees, led by Secretary Brownie, had no experience in disaster management, setting off an exodus of FEMA's most talented staffers. More than three thousand troops of the Louisiana National Guard's 256th Brigade, who hail from New Orleans and southern Louisiana, could have helped immediately. Instead, they were forced to watch New Orleans drown on TV like the rest of us, from their bunkers in another Gulf wasteland, Iraq.

ABC News reported that two days before Katrina hit New Orleans, the White House did receive detailed damage forecasts from Homeland Security officials predicting that the city's levees might be overtopped or breached. Did the vacationing Bush miss these warnings or ignore them? According to Senator Joseph Lieberman, the White House refused to answer that question. "Almost every question our staff has asked federal agency witnesses regarding conversations with or involvement of the White House has been met with a response that they could not answer, on direction of the White House," said Lieberman. If these warnings had been heeded, people could have been evacuated before the storm hit and additional resources could have been put in place. Bush didn't bother to think about the 100,000 New Orleanians who didn't have their own car to get out of town.

At some point, incompetence, insensitivity, and stupidity cease being viable excuses for Bush. Whenever you look at Bush's disasters, there is a pattern of not only blithely ignoring warnings but also taking proactive steps that make the looming catastrophe even more terrible. Bush cut funds, passed laws, and changed long-standing organizational structures before every one of the catastrophes that happened on his watch, ensuring that the meltdown would be even more monumental. Besides New Orleans and the 2008 financial crisis, look at 9/11. Bush claimed that no one could have anticipated those levees being breached either. The claim was that our air defenses were still on a Cold War footing, pointed "outwards" to guard against a Soviet attack, and not "inwards" to deal with hijackings of commercial airliners. This is a complete lie, of course—the United States did have established and routinely executed protocols for dealing with even the slightest possibility of a hijacked aircraft for decades, until June 1, 2001. That day was when Bush and Rumsfeld subtly changed the hijacking protocols, so that instead of local air traffic controllers being able to request assistance directly from the military, they now had to seek authorization from the secretary of Defense. During a critical period on the morning of 9/11, Rumsfeld was unable to be contacted. And besides the famous President's Daily Brief entitled "Bin Laden Determined to Strike Inside U.S." that Bush ignored, consider the fact that he also pre-emptively ordered U.S. intelligence agents to "back off" on investigating both bin Laden and the Saudi royal family soon after he took office, as reported by the BBC.

You see, Bush welcomes disasters. They're very profitable for his pals in the "reconstruction" business, who don't actually reconstruct anything, but get paid anyway. Halliburton didn't just win billions to pretend to rebuild Iraq, they won billions to pretend to rebuild New Orleans, too. More than three years after the disaster, thousands of refugees of Hurricane Katrina are still living in toxic FEMA camping trailers, made out of cheap composite wood that emits carcinogenic formaldehyde vapors in the Louisiana heat.

Infrastructure Concerns
What are the probabilities on what will collapse next?

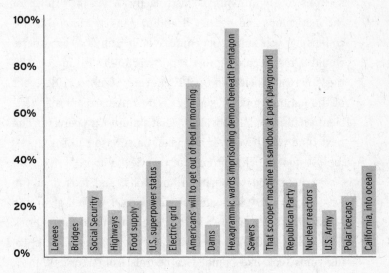

The levees of New Orleans were the most egregious example of Bush's indifference and criminally misplaced priorities in protecting our nation's infrastructure, but it is by no means the only one. The Bush-era memories of Americans across the country feature plenty of rubble, twisted girders, blackouts, and body bags. National security expert Stephen Flynn put it well in the August 2, 2007, issue of *Popular Mechanics:* "The fact is that Americans have been squandering the infrastructure legacy bequeathed to us by earlier generations. Like the spoiled offspring of well-off parents, we behave as though we have no idea what is required to sustain the quality of our daily lives." Who does that remind you of?

There was the catastrophic failure of the busy I-35 bridge that collapsed into the Mississippi River in Minneapolis on August 1, 2007, killing 13 people and injuring 145. There have been several metaphors employed throughout this book comparing the Bush years to driving off a cliff; perhaps I was subconsciously thinking of this tragedy. When the bridges of the meticulous and orderly Scandinavians of Minnesota are collapsing, you know this country is in trouble. The experts would agree; according to a report card released in 2005 by the American Society of Civil Engineers, 160,570 bridges out of the nation's total of 590,750 were rated structurally deficient or functionally obsolete. That's almost 27 percent. The next time you drive over a bridge, be sure to rub that lucky rabbit's-foot dangling from your rearview mirror.

I happened to be in Minneapolis, and looked at the I-35 bridge a few days after it collapsed. I walked along the Mississippi River, where a stretch of old, tumbled-down, brick flour mills and docks have been turned into a park. The hulking ruins look like bombed cathedrals from World War II.

Scattered groups of disaster-sightseers were clustered near the riverbank. I joined them to look across the river at the newly destroyed infrastructure. The cracked bridge ramped downward at sickening, broken angles. Rescue boats floated around chunks of the bridge. You couldn't walk downriver and get too close; the area was still blocked off by police and emergency vehicles. It reminded me of when I went into work in Manhattan on September 12, 2001, to *The Onion* office at 10th Avenue and 20th Street. I looked down that broad, west-side avenue, past the police barricade. There were endless rows of hundreds of red-and-white ambulances, parked on both sides and all the way down the street, receding into the distance as far as the eye could see. All of the vehicles were pointed downtown, where the World Trade Towers had dominated the skyline twenty-four hours earlier, now replaced by a pillar of black smoke. When I think back upon the Bush years, I'll always remember shuffling slowly past a variety of disaster zones.

There was the Northeast Blackout of August 14, 2003—at the time, the most widespread electrical blackout in history, affecting forty million Americans in eight states. Here in New York City, the Capital of the World, the City That Never Sleeps, it was as pitch black as a campground in the middle of the woods that night. The only sources of illumination were the weak, bobbing flashlights of people wandering slowly down the sidewalks, treating themselves to the free ice cream that the delis had put out from their nonworking freezers. You know, that is one nice thing that Bush gave us—a couple of half-melted ice cream bars that we could suck on in the darkness. Thanks for that, George, sincerely. We were told that the cause of the blackout was untrimmed trees in Ohio brushing into a power line, which set off a cascading chain reaction of outages. It's more likely that Bush was still listening to his best pal in prison, Ken Lay, and had tried to stick the entire national power grid into a single circuit breaker.

Oh yeah, Enron. It was a more innocent time, those last few months of 2001, when only one gigantic corporation was going bankrupt because of massive fraud and corruption, instead of one after another after another. Let's put those Enron tapes inside our Bush time capsule to warn future generations, on which you can listen to Enron traders agree to "get a little creative and come up with a reason" to shut down power plants, in order to create artificial energy shortages and drive up prices. While California was getting hit with rolling blackouts and billions of dollars in surcharges, Enron officials laughed on tape about how they were "stealing" obscene amounts of money *every day* from California and fleecing "Grandma Millie" to bring in record profits.

The lesson that was learned from Enron is that the privatization of our national infrastructure into the hands of cock-lords like Ken Lay is something that we should never allow again. Of course, Bush was best friends with this cock-lord, so this lesson went right over his head. Another collaborator, Mitch Daniels, Bush's former budget director and now the governor of Indiana, signed a deal in 2006 to turn over operation of the 157-mile Indiana Toll Road to a private Spanish/Australian foreign corporate consortium for the next seventy-five years. Now we're not just handing over our infrastructure to corrupt U.S. corporations, we're throwing it overseas to foreigners. Make sure you have a lot of one-euro coins and kangaroo quarters on hand to pay those jacked-up tolls. But don't worry, if you're driving through Indiana and suddenly your car disappears down a gigantic sinkhole that

Consumer Protections

Although George W. Bush often spoke of his duty to keep Americans safe, a closer look at his record on consumer safety suggests that he may actually want all of us dead.

Protection	Bush's Deregulation	Bush's Intent
Olestra labeling	Dropped requirement to label foods containing olestra, including a warning of health risks	Just enjoys making Americans shit their pants, through phony terror alerts or synthesized sucrose molecules with ester-linked fatty acids
Tire-pressure monitoring	Weakened standards to warn drivers of underinflated tires	Identify the homosexual communists who actually care about something like tire pressure
Medical privacy standards	Health care providers now do not need to obtain patients' consent before sharing medical records	Alert health insurance companies on which patients might actually make them pay out money for health care
Driving hours for truckers	Increased the hours a trucker can drive in one work shift	Provide more dramatic accident scenes of twisted wreckage to entertain motorists during long, boring drives
Ability to file class-action lawsuits in state courts	Class-action lawsuits must now be brought to federal court, where they will not be heard	Protect corporations from being held accountable for their scams, defective and dangerous products, pollution, and other frivolous claims
Nursing home care	Dropped training requirements for workers who feed nursing home patients	Reduce the number of useless eaters
Rat poison safeguards for children	Manufacturers now not required to include a bittering agent and an indicator dye that makes it apparent that a child ate rat poison	Rat infestation more common in urban, largely African-American and Latino neighborhoods, so, you know, whatever
Limiting use of carcinogenic weed killer atrazine	Increased maximum level of atrazine allowed in public drinking water 12 times over; put atrazine's manufacturer in charge of monitoring contamination of drinking water	Use of atrazine more common in suburban, largely white neighborhoods with lawns, so, you know, whatever

gapes open in that foreign-owned highway, just call the corporate help line in Madrid or Sydney. If you can speak Spanish or Australian, they'll do their best to get someone out there to help you in a few weeks.

Walking through the streets of old, dilapidated New York City feels like traversing a minefield lately. There was the underground steam pipe explosion in Midtown Manhattan on July 18, 2007, when a geyser of boiling steam over 1,000 feet high burst out of a busy intersection, ripping open a 35-foot-wide crater and raining down chunks of asphalt and mud on fleeing pedestrians. (In his last deregulation push, Bush tried to increase the maximum pressure allowed in steam pipes.) Many pet dogs—and in 2004, a woman walking her dog—have been electrocuted to death when they stepped on a metal plate in the street that was coursing with stray voltage. Make sure you have a nice, thick rubber sole on your shoes. Keep your eye on the sky, too, as construction cranes have been collapsing with alarming regularity. Most of the planet's newest and largest construction cranes lately are in Dubai, building skyscrapers in the shape of a starfish, so we get the old, shitty cranes now. And still, eight years after 9/11, we haven't managed to build a thing at Ground Zero. Once a year, they shoot a light beam into the sky at night to honor those who lost their lives in the tragedy, but every other day of the year, all we have is a big, sad hole. The subway trains roll through the darkened, grimy, garbage-strewn old World Trade Center station, slowing enough for you to look through the windows and take it all in. The price of a subway fare keeps going up, but they still can't fix this awful, daily reminder of both our president's failure to protect us and his complete indifference to helping us rebuild.

Of course, we can't expect the president to be out there on his hands and knees, checking every rivet on every bridge and every valve on the steam pipes. What we expect is that our president should disperse the necessary funds, which we give him, to make sure that we remain a modern, functioning civilization. Instead, we get Bush's new disaster capitalism, as Naomi Klein so ably points out in her new book, *The Shock Doctrine*. Instead of federally funded reconstruction, we get private corporations who grab huge federal contracts, then do nothing. They still can't keep the lights on, pick up the garbage, or keep the sewers flowing in Baghdad, after we've spent $3 trillion on Bush's pointless war. Will it take ferocious geysers of human excrement exploding from our manholes to make us realize how much money Bush has flushed down the toilet in Iraq?

Besides our deteriorating bridges, roads, trains, airports, and sewer systems, our national safety net has not been safe under Bush either. Remember how he wanted to privatize Social Security and throw all of our money on the roulette wheel of the stock market? Thank Christ he didn't succeed on that one. But one quote by Bush captures how excited he was about the prospect of taking the money we pay with every single paycheck, in order to provide for us all when we are old and frail, and giving it to the corrupt crooks of Wall Street. Before September 11, 2001, Bush pledged to never crack open the Social Security lockbox, except in the event of recession, war, or a national emergency. But after "everything changed" on 9/11, Bush couldn't contain his glee. A few days after we were plunged into that recession, war, and national emergency, Bush gloated to his good old budget director Mitch Daniels regarding Social Security, "Lucky me—I hit the trifecta!" For those of you who haven't been out to the horse track in a while, the trifecta is when you correctly bet on which horse will finish first, second, and third. You win a big pot of money if you get all three right. Bush thought this joke was so funny that he repeated it at more than a dozen Republican campaign luncheons, all the way through 2002. If this had been an off-the-cuff wisecrack that Bush had said once, perhaps we could let this slide—"Oh, that's just our rascally, frat-boy president trying to be funny. Don't mind him!" But Bush liked his own joke so much that he made it into a catchphrase for a full year. This says it all. A few days after three thousand Americans were killed in the most gruesome ways imaginable, while the black smoke hung in the air over New York City and rescue workers were digging body parts out of the mountain of wreckage that Lower Manhattan had become, Bush felt "lucky" that he could exploit this catastrophe in order to steal our national savings that we'd all spent our working lifetimes to build. Just for this one joke alone, we as a nation have the sacred duty to ensure that Bush spends his retirement living in a piss-drenched cardboard box on the streets of Washington, D.C., eating rotten garbage out of Dumpsters. Dick Cheney shouldn't even get a box.

EARTH: LOVE IT OR LEAVE IT

Is It Me, or Is the Globe Getting Warmer?

O h, the environment. The poor, poor environment. The slow death of our planet is just not as dramatic and thrilling as the War on Terror. It doesn't get the same media coverage. There're no dramatic attacks and counterattacks, no daring captures and escapes, no heroes and villains; just villains—the corporate polluters who quietly poison us all. Bush has given us some long-term memories to deal with, by poisoning our public resources to make quick, easy profits for his private pals. Bush never came up with a good enemy to pin his War on the Environment on, like a particularly scary shark or killer virus. So he just secretly dumps pig shit into our drinking water while we're not looking.

Instead of public service, the environmental and consumer-safety appointees of the Bush administration have been dedicated to the dicking-over of the public. They were led on this sacred mission by the creeds of deregulation and privatization. Come on, would you really trust these kinds of guys to keep your lights on, to keep your water supply safe, and to keep poisons out of your food? These guys don't care about you. They don't have time for you. They don't have time for anybody. Even if you were best friends with one of these guys at your country club, would you trust him to come over and water your houseplants while you were on vacation? With their incredible touch for neglect and catastrophe, your ficus plant would probably shed its dry, withered leaves directly into an electrical outlet, igniting a blaze that would consume your entire house in a roaring fireball. Then you would learn that your friend had somehow taken out a $10 million insurance policy on your house, and was now on a plane to a luxury golf resort in Fiji.

"Good-bye, from the world's biggest polluter!"

—George W. Bush, in parting words to British Prime Minister Gordon Brown and French President Nicolas Sarkozy at his final G8 Summit, punching the air and grinning widely as the two leaders looked at him in shock, July 10, 2008

George W. Bush is the remorseless, joyful leader of this Skull-and-Bones-frat-boys-gone-wild crew. They're like the Deltas from *Animal House,* on crack. Bush promised to toilet-paper the trees of every forest and to put a flaming bag of dog shit in front of every wildlife habitat. They might get us all kicked off campus by the Dean of the Universe one of these days.

We were told that George W. Bush came to Washington as a uniter, ready to tackle big issues like the environment with his large, kind ears—and he certainly did. Setting aside party ideologues and his own preconceptions, our president listened to his gut. Bush's twisted bowels grumbled out an environmental policy designed to reach across deep divides, in a way that all people could easily understand and identify with. The message was simple: There's too much environment in people's lives, and we need to come together to do something about it.

From the former coal-industry big shots in the safety-regulation departments, to the company that just wanted to quietly go about the business of selling its weed-killer atrazine (a by-product of which is hermaphroditic frogs), to the guy who was sick of his neighbors bitching at him about burning tires, Bush's environmental policy instantly made perfect sense. You have to slash and burn your own way through this world. The environment can't do everything for you, Bush said, and everyone who stood to benefit from that statement wholeheartedly agreed.

Mining companies came together and started wildly cutting the tops off of the Appalachian Mountains in West Virginia to share things we can all have in common—coal and black lung disease. Industrial farms agreed to share their wastewater, allowing their fecal reservoirs to overflow into local water systems. Today, nearby citizens can all simply wait fifteen minutes after pouring a glass of water, so that the pig shit has time to settle to the bottom of the glass. It wasn't just big polluters, asthma sufferers, and people who enjoy the taste of pig shit who benefited. There was something for everyone. Even those who could afford to buy a new Hummer benefited from Bush's unifying theory on the environment by using a massive tax loophole he created to help them write off its entire cost. Bush left it up to every American to decide how he or she could exploit the environment best.

Ever the uniter, Bush also didn't let the environment

Environmental Deregulation

George W. Bush presided over an unprecedented rollback of environmental protections. Here are several key issues, the deregulation that Bush supported, and the reasoning for Bush's stance, which has nothing to do with lining the pockets of his corporate supporters.

Issue	Deregulation	Bush's Reasoning
Dredging and filling wetlands	Eased requirements for replacing wetlands destroyed by mining	Wetlands could be infiltrated by Iraq's Marsh Arabs
Arctic National Wildlife Refuge	Pushed to open 1.5 million acres of Arctic Refuge to oil drilling	Hollywood's CGI-animated penguins and polar bears have become sufficiently realistic
Mercury emissions	Revoked a determination that mercury emissions are hazardous	People driven mad by mercury poisoning are hilarious
Coal dust standards	Increased the allowable level of coal dust in mines	We must ensure employment opportunities for America's canaries
Roadless areas on forest land	Opened up 60 million acres of national forest to logging	U.S. can restore its economy by converting its forests into chopsticks for the Chinese
Cleanup at oil drilling sites	Made previously mandatory cleanup optional for oil and gas companies	Freedom of choice is for all Americans (except women)
Grizzly bear habitat	Opened grizzly bear habitat to snowmobiles	Grizzlies are murderous beasts that love to kill Americans; they must be pushed back before they conquer us
Mountaintop mining	Made it easier for mining companies to dump rubble into rivers	More rubble in rivers makes for more exciting whitewater rafting
Radioactive waste disposal from nuclear power plants	Permitted radioactive waste to be disposed of in ordinary landfills instead of closely monitored facilities	Americans need extra eyeballs to become even more vigilant against terrorism

dictate our response to 9/11, when he told the public that the air quality around Ground Zero was safe. We all remember how the Bush administration came together and provided a united front to tell those living/dying near Ground Zero that the air quality was perfectly fine, and that it just happened to be nose-bleed season. No alarming environmental data about the air quality after 9/11 was going to hold Bush hostage. Can you really blame the Environmental Protection Agency for obeying Bush's order to lie, with the toxic clouds of doom in the sky and their pH test strips spontaneously combusting? Bush instead chose to protect us from that data, which would have been a serious downer after everything else that had happened. After all, people needed to come to Ground Zero. People needed to breathe the air filled with dangerous toxins. People went. People saw. People got sick. People got mad that they got sick. Luckily, Bush didn't puff a bunch of CO_2 into the air with apologies. He just cut the medical benefits for 9/11 first responders. Our president always stood behind the people who stood united against the environment, and its various inhabitants. He also made sure to remind the EPA who's boss by cutting $600 million from the agency's budget.

Seeing the opportunity to link a catastrophic national security crisis with domestic policy designed to enact sound changes that would propel us into an era of clean energy from being enacted, Bush kept uniting. Those in the business of operating aging power plants responded to his sympathetic gutting of clean-air standards by ignoring the twenty thousand premature deaths each year that this would cause, and standing firmly alongside the president in his belief that the terrorists would be smoked out.

Ever since Bush eliminated EPA regulations for air

quality, it has become increasingly more terrifying to look up in the skies. For instance, that swirling green vortex leading to another dimension never used to be there. Air quality has gotten so bad that Philip Morris has begun to collect royalties after winning a lawsuit against the atmosphere for copyright infringement. Bush's approach to air pollution was often suspect, like the time he tried to buy a million air fresheners for the nation from Wal-Mart. And who could forget when Bush got tough on mercury emissions by chasing after a cloud with a tennis racket? Perhaps the first sign that Bush meant to change the nation's overall stance on air pollution came when the anti-pollution spokesbird, Woodsy the Owl, had a puff of smoke coming out of his mouth every time he hooted. Bush even went so far as to change Smokey the Bear's motto to "Only You Can Mind Your Own Business." At least he got tough on the most-pollution-emitting factories when he called for minimum height requirements on all smokestacks. Bush's "You Must Be This Tall to Pollute" campaign proved to be the most effective environmental program of his administration.

Our killer duck president tried to get the gray wolf off the list of endangered species before he left office. He also tried to have several other animals decertified as endangered, or has proposed incentives for hunting them. This includes the Controlling America's Donkeys act, the bonobo monkeys who are notorious for sharing, the chimpanzees, which share DNA markers with him, the soft and friendly manatees who refuse to patrol our shores and defeat foreign terror threats, and the too-clever-for-their-own-good dolphins. Bush also wanted to change the Republican mascot from an elephant, since the elephant's memory is too long for today's pro-amnesia GOP. He proposed changing it to a raccoon, to symbolize the scrappy, thieving, trash-eating spirit of Dubya.

Although Bush did everything he could to our national park system, many are still standing. You can't really blame a guy for trying to do away with a bunch of land that animals are just using to poop on. After all, what have any of those species done to better themselves over the last eight years? Did they read picture books to children, or meet with a ton of stupid foreign leaders who never shut up about stuff? No, they didn't. According to government records, no members of the U.S. fauna have pulled themselves up by their bootstraps. That is why Bush has fought so diligently to prevent unemployed animals from living for free off of government welfare. Bush has pushed to make the residents of our national parks accountable, by creating jobs so the working animals can earn their keep. Unfortunately, many of the squirrels, raccoons, and bears hired to work in national park gift shops were fired for biting, clawing, and mauling customers. Sadly, the flora living in the parks did even less—mostly just standing there and dropping leaves.

The first budget report from the Bush administration was also the first one in history with photographs, many of them featuring Dubya clearing brush or breathing crisp, fresh mountain air through his mouth. These outdoorsy photos of Bush enjoying the environment appeared right next to lines of text that cut funding for national parks and gave subsidies to polluters. Some photos that were produced for the budget publication, such as Bush dancing with oil-slicked penguins, or tenderly nursing orphaned baby Arctic seals, were rejected as excessively obvious propaganda.

There are certain species of wildlife that Bush does value. In order to unite with Syngenta, the manufacturer of the top-selling weed-killer atrazine, Bush defended the hermaphroditic frogs that this carcinogenic chemical produced. Bush vowed to preserve the sanctity of life for every young frog chick with a dick, as well as to protect our nation's fragile, amphibious mangina regions. Syngenta thanked Bush for deregulating atrazine into our drinking water supply by creating a new media mascot to raise awareness on this issue: Francis, the Hermaphroditic Frog. It is predicted that this cartoon character will be wildly popular with our oncoming generation of hermaphroditic children. Bush targeted not only our public resources for private gain, but also our pubic resources.

The whales could use a bailout. The rain forest could use a bailout. The great apes urgently need a bailout, but it was the *Homo destructus* species of the Wall Street freako-system who got bailed out with $700 billion from Bush. Then again, have you seen the mansions in Greenwich, Connecticut, where these hairless hedge fund apes live? Have you witnessed the verdant, emerald glory of their expansive lawns? That's a lot of precious greenery that needs mowing, edging, and shrub-trimming, if you want to keep your alpha males happy. Bush made sure that the Mexican-coordinated preservation of our financiers' private estates would never wither away. If Obama ends up bailing out the Big Three automakers in Detroit, they'd better agree to only make cars that run on peanut butter and smiles from now on.

Bush was a strong proponent of the Clear America's Skies Act, which would have authorized the Blue Angels to clear the skies of birds with Sidewinder missiles and depleted-uranium

Gatling guns. George simply wanted to make sure that the skies were always clear above every ranch-based ecosystem in America. In fact, Bush authorized the renaming of all other ecosystems as *ranches* in late 2008. A lake is now a *wet-ranch,* a federally protected wetland is a *swamp-ranch,* and mountainous areas are now *rock-ranches.* Hiking has been renamed *hill-ranching,* and swimming is *aqua-ranching.* Playing fetch with your dog is called *yard-wrangling.* Unfortunately, hidden in Bush's ranch-renaming bill was a decree that all U.S. ranches are immune to pollution laws and legally belong to Texans.

Our president has singlehandedly done more harm to the environment, which Bush claims may not exist (he may

Bush's Alternative Energy Proposals

Which ecologically sustainable energy sources did President Bush support? Here is the 2009 federal budget to develop alternative energy, with dollar amounts in millions.

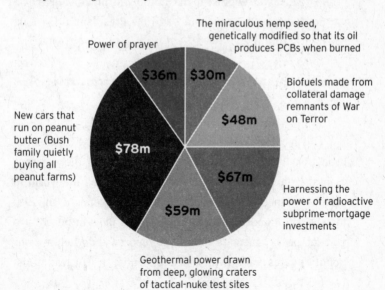

Power of prayer

The miraculous hemp seed, genetically modified so that its oil produces PCBs when burned

$36m $30m

$48m

Biofuels made from collateral damage remnants of War on Terror

New cars that run on peanut butter (Bush family quietly buying all peanut farms)

$78m

$67m

$59m

Harnessing the power of radioactive subprime-mortgage investments

Geothermal power drawn from deep, glowing craters of tactical-nuke test sites

soon be right), than any other person, group, or smokestack. By reaching across the aisle of Congress and bonking politicians' heads together, Bush was able to create tax loopholes for SUVs nearly as large as the holes in the ozone, or the holes forming in Americans' oxygen-deprived brains. Thankfully, Americans can join Bush and put their minds at ease. With Bush's complete tax write-offs on brand new Hummers, which can easily fit eight full-grown assholes and their four fat fuck kids, there was no reason for everyone to pile into the vehicle all at once. In fact, everyone in the family could have had their very own Hummer, if Bush had not warned us that our nation is facing the significant danger of running out of decent parking spaces. Bush, who considers himself a compassionate conservationist, also asked Americans not to waste gasoline by allowing their vehicles to idle, rather than turning them on and off all the time. Leading by example, Bush issued standing orders to keep the engines in his motorcade, his *Air Force One* jet, his *Marine One* helicopter, and his Presidential Go-Kart constantly running.

"We need an energy bill that encourages consumption."
—George W. Bush, Trenton, New Jersey, September 23, 2002

Bush, determined to keep facts outside of EPA reports, brought a Washington outsider perspective to the environmental organization. In fact, the agency has led the world in omissions since 2001. With a keen focus on oversight, the EPA managed to quadruple omissions of hard facts in nearly 100 percent of the agency's published reports, thus helping our pollution rates reach an all-time best. Under the Bush administration, the EPA found ways to circumvent air standards better than any nation on the planet. Bush was always on the lookout for ways to conserve resources. For example, he refused to sign the Kyoto Protocol, as it would have been a waste of perfectly good ink.

When billions of innocents were sentenced to consecutive Bush terms, they were told there was no proof of global warming. Was George W. Bush just being ignorant, or was it an elaborate plan by Karl Rove to encourage a sweaty Bush to take off his shirt and pants? This would explain why the White House stereo was always blasting the Nelly single "Hot in Herre." Could Rove have tricked a grown man, who attended the finest Ivy League colleges, into running around in his undies? Not only does it seem possible, Rove probably also convinced the president that global warming didn't exist by frequently using ice cubes to cool off the president's searing nipples. Psychologists say that those who were molested often block out and forget large amounts of information. It all kind of makes sense then.

Bush's absolute refusal to back solar panel energy is baffling, but according to interviews with Barbara Bush, her son has always been adamantly opposed to the entire spectrum of solar light. As a toddler, he would spend most of his days inside the deepest, darkest tunnels of the Bush family nest. Little George came out only when his mother served up a breakfast of her famous egg sacs. Still, if we can get skin cancer from sitting outside in the sun for five minutes, shouldn't we somehow harness all that power? Is Bush worried that our solar power could fall into the hands of terrorists? For once, Bush might be using foresight. If an enemy of America harnessed solar energy and focused a giant beam of light through a massive orbital magnifying glass, they could easily burn us to a crisp like ants.

Despite his campaign promises, Bush went back on his word by declaring that rock 'n' roll was noise pollution. Luckily, a group of hard-rockin' kids with a bass-playing dune buggy convinced Congress not to pass the bill. It would all be so much funnier if we didn't have only this one planet to live on. Bush's real broken promise to send a man to Mars was among his most disappointing. That looked like it was going to be the only way to avoid being on the same planet as George W. Bush—a very dangerous prospect, indeed.

OUR ECONOMY—
NOSEDIVING
LIKE AN EAGLE

The Welfare Queens of Wall Street

Whenever Bush stumbled out in his rouge and lipstick to deliver a direct address to the American people on prime-time TV, you knew it was going to be bad. On September 24, 2008, when Bush appeared on TV to shake us down for the $700 billion financial bailout, he looked dazed and heavily made up, as if he had just been hit by a Maybelline truck. The masters of Wall Street knew that if they wanted to frighten the American people into bailing them out, all they had to do was trot out that little gremlin in front of the cameras. Have him look right into the camera and say the chilling words "My fellow Americans . . ." Shit, what now?!? The country is under attack again? Oh, you want a kajillion dollars of our money for Wall Street? Fine! Give us further updates on the radio, we'll be hiding down in the root cellar! *Just make George W. Bush stop talking!*

Bush gave us no time to think about this one. He gave

our sleep-deprived congressional representatives the chance to read, comprehend, and debate a 442-page slab of legislation in twenty-four hours. Why not stand them upright in a tiny concrete cell, with their limbs shackled to an iron hook in the floor, and staple the bill right to their eyeballs? That should help their concentration. "So, are you ready to sign that bailout bill yet?" Bush could ask through the barred window at the crack of dawn.

The amazing part was that our House of Representatives, under enormous pressure from their alarmed constituents, actually rejected the no-oversight bailout initially. So Bush came right back at them a few days later, threatened several representatives with martial law, and got his bailout passed. This is our money that Bush sucked away, and we have no say in the matter. Bush might as well just finish the job on us before he leaves office. He could shave our heads, stick us into pods filled with gelatinous liquid, and start harvesting our body heat energy.

Bush told us that the bailout money was needed to buy certain "troubled assets" of banks, so that they could start lending money again and resume the flow of credit to consumers and businesses. If the flow of credit was not restored, Bush imagineered for us the "financial panic" and "distressing scenario" and "painful and lasting damage" that would unfold: closed banks and businesses, lost jobs, plummeting home values, and wiped-out retirement accounts. What Bush didn't tell us is that 10 percent of the bailout—yeah, that's $70 *billion*—would be headed straight into the silk-lined pockets of Wall Street executives, the people who peddled these "troubled assets," in the form of salaries and bonuses. This is why we had to rush

Dow Jones Industrial Average, 2001–2008

How has the stock market fared during President Bush's tenure?

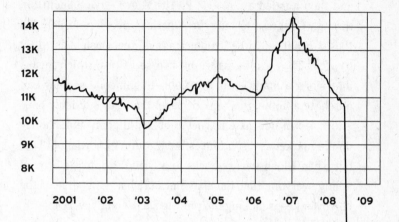

the money to them, with no planning or oversight? These guys really didn't have enough money in their checking accounts to make it through the end of the month? You know, top executives on Wall Street make only about $400 million a year; you'd be surprised how quickly they can go through that. These are the men who drove the financial system to the brink of collapse through their greed and fraud, and Bush made us give them fucking *bonuses*. It's just like 9/11, when Bush pinned medals on the chests of the military commanders who failed to protect us. In Bush's America, right up until the end, one maxim held true: the greater the failure, the greater the reward.

> **"This is an impressive crowd—the haves and the have-mores. Some people call you the elites; I call you my base."**
>
> —George W. Bush, to a crowd of cackling, diamond-studded plutocrats at an $800-a-plate dinner, October 20, 2000

Sticking to his 9/11 script, Bush ignored obvious warnings about the approaching economic crisis, let everything blow up, and then hustled a massive, PATRIOT Act–style bailout bill through Congress to hurt the American people and help his "base." What are these "troubled assets" that Bush insisted we pay for? They are mortgage-backed securities, which means that when a bank lends $100,000 to someone so they can purchase a home, the bank declares that they suddenly have $300,000 in new assets. They then sell this invisible money on the market as a solid investment. I don't know about you, but when I loan twenty bucks to a friend, I don't go around telling everyone that I'm sixty bucks richer. Of course, if the borrower keeps making their mortgage payment every month, with interest, over many years that bank's debt *will* turn into wealth. But what if mortgage lenders use predatory tactics to entice consumers into taking on home loans, such as misrepresenting the terms of loans, making loans without regard to consumers' ability to repay, making loans with deceptive "teaser" rates that later balloon astronomically, packing loans with undisclosed charges and fees, or even paying illegal kickbacks? Those consumers will *not* be able to pay back those loans, which means that the mortgage-backed securities that Wall Street sold are worth nothing. That's what our $700 billion bought: nothing. And we're even paying the full price for this nothing, the original price that the banks pretended these securities were worth, instead of the actual current value of these securities, which, again, is nothing.

Guess who enabled these predatory lending practices? Yeah, you know who. Eliot Spitzer, the former governor of New York, put it right in the headline of his article in the *Washington Post* on February 14, 2008: "Predatory Lenders'

Desperate Times for Banks

What are the most popular enticements that banks are now offering to attract new account holders?

1	A shoulder to cry on, available Monday to Thursday, 9 am to 2 pm
2	New extra-glossy brochures, featuring more attractive stock-photo models
3	Free lollipops for adults, as well as children
4	For all account balances over $5,000, bank president will mow your lawn once a week
5	The Cashback Rebate Low-Rate Rewards Passport Super Savers Club, which can actually earn you money! (Cost: $54.99/month)
6	Rock-solid guarantee that bank's chief financial officers will never use your savings to pay for spa massage sessions, unless their tennis elbow is really acting up
7	Brand-new toaster (made in China)
8	Emergency cyanide capsule (made in China)
9	For single women: marriage proposal
10	For single men: legally binding fuck-buddy agreement

Source: *How Small Banks Can Avoid Tanking Straight Down the Toilet*, www.fdic.gov

Partner in Crime—How the Bush Administration Stopped the States from Stepping In to Help Consumers." Spitzer tried to warn us of this impending crisis by detailing how Bush negated laws in 2003 (which had been in place since the 1860s) that protected consumers from predatory lenders. As payback for alerting the nation to Bush's connivance with lenders to victimize consumers, Spitzer got himself torpedoed by his bombshell of a prostitute one month later and was forced to resign in shame. It's safe to say that every politician has a skeleton (or a voluptuous young woman) in their closets. Consider George W. Bush's avoidance of war duty in Vietnam and his mysterious one-year vacation from the Texas Air National Guard, his cocaine abuse and DUI arrest, or why exactly male prostitute Jeff "Bulldog" Gannon, with no journalistic credentials, was given unprecedented access as a reporter to the White House from 2003 to 2005. The real question is, if and when will the scandal be revealed? If you try to tell the truth, blow a whistle, or ring an alarm bell, like that hard-charging horn-dog Spitzer did, it's safe to say that you will be retaliated against by the powerful people you're exposing, for a moment when you were not so squeaky clean.

So Bush not only ignored the warnings, but actively helped to create the subprime mortgage crisis. Then he got the chance to raid our Treasury for one last big score, which he passed out to his favorite "haves and have-mores." But still, thank God that we bailed out the high-finance companies. If we hadn't, we all would have been huddled around trash-can fires, trying to stay warm, just like Bush said, right? I'm sure that the executives of the insurance giant AIG were grateful that our nation's financial collapse was averted. A week after AIG solemnly received $85 billion of taxpayers' money, they soberly considered how to get our nation's economy back on track during a weeklong retreat for their top sales agents at the luxurious St. Regis resort in Monarch Beach, California. Expenses for the week totaled $442,000, including $200,000 for hotel rooms, $150,000 for food, and $23,000 in spa charges. Ah, lovely Monarch Beach. It's the only place where a monarch can truly unwind, far away from the peasants who paid for his trip there.

These Wall Street overlords, these "masters of the universe," these mighty kings of Castle Grayskull, supposedly knew what they were doing. In the infinitely complex system of the free market, they were the wise leaders who were powering America into a new golden age—just like the Bush team, which was heralded as "the CEO administration" that would run like clockwork, as opposed to the all-night pizza-and-blowjob binges of the Clinton years. We were fooled by these men, with their air of authority, their expensive wristwatches, shimmering neckties, and rich, dark suits. Now, these masters of the universe lie helpless on the floor, with their hollow rubber heads caved in, their grotesquely inflated bodies smudged and chipped, and their tiny weapons lost under the couch. They're not good for anything, except perhaps for inserting firecrackers into their torsos and trying to melt their heads off in one last attempt at entertainment. Our kids don't even play with all-American He-Man toys anymore. They like those new Asian toys like Pokémon and Bakugan nowadays.

Wall Street traders in fact have a different brain physiognomy than normal humans. Their swollen hindbrains are much more developed than their forebrains. The primeval, rudimentary, reptilian part of our brain, with the sole purpose of accumulating more and eating more, to become fatter, stronger, and more powerful, takes up most of the average financier's cranial capacity. The forebrain's purposes of empathy, foresight, and caution are absent. The financiers are a parasite class—they don't produce anything of value themselves. They only figure out how to suck more money out of every other industry. Look at what they did to health care.

Rising from the torrent of bad news about our financial collapse, there is one story that warms the heart. According to CNBC, the chief executive of Lehman Brothers, Richard Fuld—let's call him Dick—was running on a treadmill in the Lehman Brothers corporate gym on September 21, 2008, when news of Lehman Brothers' bankruptcy appeared on a television screen. Some guy who was pumping iron in the corner walked over to Dick Fuld and punched him right in his vulture face. "Knocked him out cold" is the direct quote. After millions of stories of violence committed against the powerless, this is one act of violence that can bring a smile to our faces. What if all of the American workers who have watched their retirement savings evaporate got the chance to punch the CEOs of their brokerage firms? Not all at the same time, of course—beating people to death isn't very nice. This isn't Italy in 1945 quite yet. But if just one punch could be dished out per day, that would be appropriate. I'm sure there would be a line of thousands of people patiently waiting their turn outside each CEO's mansion to take their shot. This system of daily punches would go a long way toward reestablishing American citizens' faith in their financial system. There could be a ferry that would take investors to the private islands owned by men like Dick Fuld. These billionaires can accept their one punch a day, then they can go back to enjoying their sumptuous meals, fine liquors, hand-rolled cigars, and elite prostitutes that we paid for.

Jim Watson/AFP/Getty Images

Bush joins his three ceremonial husbands in a traditional Saudi money dance.

Spencer Platt/Getty Images

The financial markets of the world begin to melt down into a warm puddle of goo.

The American myth of Horatio Alger that used to fool us—the plucky young boy who rose from poverty to affluence through thrift, honesty, and above all, hard work—has been replaced by the seductive Powerball myth of the stock market. There's no hard work involved—you simply buy a ticket and scrape away a bit of gray film with your fingernail. But oh boy, you might just get lucky, and that five seconds of work you put in with your fingernail might net you $10 million! They tell us that anyone can buy a ticket to this cheap carnival game, but, in fact, the lottery's rigged. The system is set up so that the massively wealthy will accrue still more wealth, and the peasants will foot the bill to support our kings. They privately accrue all the rewards of their risks, but we, the public, pay for their failures. Broke people bail out the rich people in this country. We're paying for their Powerball tickets—$700 billion worth of them. That could buy a whole lot of beef jerky, Snapple, Marlboro Reds, and Rough Rider condoms, but no, it's all going to be spent on worthless pieces of paper that you can't eat, drink, smoke, or fuck with.

Now that's class warfare, you might say—don't attack the poor rich people! It's not class warfare to point out that 400 people in this country have more wealth than the bottom 150 million. Unless you're talking about a medium-sized high school, 400 people is not a "class"; 400 people is a secret society, and these 400 increased their wealth by $670 billion during the reign of George W. Bush. However, 150 million people could be considered a societal class. It is they who are the targets of class war, by a small, elite band of financial commandos with infinite funding and the most powerful of connections. The aftertax income of the top 1 percent of Americans rose 228 percent from the late 1970s through 2005.

For working families, their aftertax income rose 0 percent. Major American cities are now equaling the same disparity of wealth between rich and poor as cities in Africa. How bad is this going to get before we realize what is being done to the middle class in this country?

Oh yeah, the middle class. How are those folks doing, anyway? Bush, as well as Obama, McCain, and any other politician running for office, all like to butter us up for our votes while our wages are dropping and our jobs are being cut. They all make sure to flatter us, saying that Americans are the most hardworking, industrious people on the planet, and that they know America will be back on its feet again through our hard work. But are we really the most industrious people on the planet anymore? Maybe in the 1940s. What are we manufacturing nowadays—blogs? All of our factories got shipped off to the Third World years ago. Now we have Mexicans doing all the hard jobs that involve tools, muscular effort, and sunshine—the CEOs love welcoming our south-of-the-border amigos, because they don't have to pay illegal immigrants decent wages, give them health care, or worry about them voting.

Meanwhile, we're inside our homes that we can't pay for anymore, wrapped in a hallucinatory cocoon of cable TV, YouTube, NetFlix, Xbox 360, PlayStation 3, and massive multiplayer online fantasy role-playing dork-outs. Everything has become so ephemeral. More than three million of us are registered on Twitter, an instant-messaging service where we can broadcast our mundane daily activities to our friends: "At home . . . Looking for a job . . . Eating at McDonald's . . . Waiting in line at the unemployment office . . ." For those who still have jobs, it seems like fantasy football takes up about

35 percent of their work week. Advertising and marketing are huge U.S. employment sectors, where we try to convince one another to buy stuff we don't need with money we don't have, accompanied by lots of flashy, spinning colors. Everyone is a "manager" now, but what are they all managing? We put in longer hours than the Europeans, but what are we actually producing? Everything is made in China now. It seems that once we got to the top of the world, our economic leaders gave us a hearty slap on the back and said, "Take a load off, Americans! You've come a long way, baby! Have a six-pack or two, and a forty-two-inch plasma TV, and a brand-new house! You deserve it! Surround yourself in a nest of luxury, with conveniently placed cup holders and snack trays. It's Miller Time! Oh, and we'll be charging you twenty-seven percent interest on all that stuff you bought on your credit card." How long did we think this was going to last?

The bailout is looking more and more like the last grab of the wealth of this country. The same people who have been slashing wages, busting labor unions, demolishing our social safety net, jacking up health insurance costs, driving up the price of oil, and destroying American jobs to be replaced by sweatshops in the Third World finally realized there was no more money to skim off our scavenged corpse. So they just demanded that we hand over $700 billion to them straight out of the Treasury, no questions asked. Bush was eager to comply, as were Barack Obama and John McCain. How did they settle on exactly how much money they needed to take in order to "rescue our economy"? According to a Treasury spokeswoman quoted on Forbes.com regarding the $700 billion, "It's not based on any particular data point. We just wanted to choose a really large number." This bailout is a gigantic feeding

What Will the Bailout Pay For?

Notable expenditures in the U.S. Emergency Economic Stabilization Act of 2008

$20 billion
Freddie Mac's child support payments to Fannie Mae

$1 billion
Daily green-tea colonic spa treatments for AIG insurance corporation's top officers

$1.5 billion
Daily green-tea colonic spa treatments for AIG's top officers' pet poodles

$300 billion
Pay-off to China so they won't invade us

$500 billion
Inject liquidity into struggling credit market in tandem with a variety of pork-barrel expenditures for various constituencies; also known as a "hot-pork injection"

$60 billion
Broad range of golden, platinum, and diamond parachutes

$2 billion
Sidewalk-cleaning expenses around Wall Street high-rise office buildings

$40 billion
Investor confidence restoration; tell them how special they are to us; reassure them that the scary bear is just an imaginary monster who can never really hurt them

$700 billion
Purchase of banks' distressed assets including mortgage-backed securities with the intent to increase credit flow in the secondary mortgage markets and reduce potential losses of . . . ah, fuck it, just hand over your money

Source: *How YOU Can Make MILLIONS Doing NO WORK AT ALL!* by Henry Paulson

trough, just like in Iraq, when the illegal Coalition Provisional Authority under L. Paul Bremer opened up the spigots and poured out $12 billion in taxpayer money that simply disappeared. They can't even tell us where $9 billion of that money went. In fact, the man whom Bush originally appointed to serve as chief investment officer for disbursing the bailout money is one Reuben Jeffery III, who was the executive director of Bremer's kleptocracy in Baghdad. Jeffery ended up not getting the job, but you can see Bush's original impulse was the same as it's always been: to set up a free-fraud zone where a select few can steal the wealth of the many.

We can't ignore the huge drain on our economy that is Bush's war across the planet. The Iraq War alone has cost us $3 trillion. Our Defense Department sells surplus weapons at a deep discount or just gives them away to countries around the globe, so they can buy the next generation of sophisticated weapons from arms manufacturers on our dime to counter the older weapons they've scattered across the globe. The Pentagon even grabs taxpayers' money to pay for the build-up of other countries' military forces. For example, in 2003 the U.S government gave a $3.8 billion loan of our money to Poland, after an intense lobbying effort by Lockheed Martin (manufacturer of the F-16 fighter jet), to finance Poland's purchase of forty-eight Lockheed Martin F-16 fighter jets. These warplanes just happen to be manufactured in George W. Bush's home state of Texas. Yet somehow, this spiraling fountain of blood money hasn't pumped any juice into the staggering economy. Rather than pump the blood of war into the economy, Bush's wars have sucked the blood out of us. What gives, George? Does that nice, fat portfolio of Lockheed

Martin stock that you get once you leave office, which you will place with honor atop the mantel of your fake fireplace on your fake ranch, make it all worthwhile?

The Bush administration inherited a $236 billion budget surplus from Bill Clinton. Eight years later, the deficit stands at $422 billion and growing—a $658 billion swing to the negative. Bush entered office with the strongest economy in U.S. history and, in less than two years, turned every single economic indicator straight down. Bush expanded military spending by 50 percent. He shattered the record for the biggest annual deficit in our history. He set the all-time record for most foreclosures in a twelve-month period. While major corporate scandals rocked the U.S. economy throughout his time in office, Bush reduced the enforcement of corporate tax law—conducting fewer audits, imposing fewer penalties, and making no effort to prosecute corporate tax crimes. All fifty state governments are going bankrupt. Bush set the all-time record for biggest annual budget spending increases. The national debt has been bloated by $4 trillion, the biggest increase under any president in our history. It now stands at more than $9.85 trillion, a 72 percent increase courtesy of Bush. That's what happens when you grant ginormous tax cuts to the superrich and open up the Treasury to invite your well-connected cronies to loot as much as they want. The funny part is remembering all of those Republicans whose sole purpose in voting for Bush was that he wasn't one of those big-spending Democrats who didn't know how to run the economy. See you in the unemployment line, with all the rest of us. Who knows, maybe we'll get lucky and Bush will fly overhead in his presidential helicopter, unzip his pants, and trickle down some golden wealth onto our heads.

WHAT THEY
THINK OF
U.S.

The World vs. George W. Bush

T he United States is not the only country that George
W. Bush has had by the nuts for the last eight years.
Nearly every country in the world has been left
sprawled out on the ground at some point, groaning with
pain, after a swift Bush kick to their groin. Yet with the eternal
spirit of human perseverance, foreigners would painfully drag
themselves to their feet, gently cupping their bruised genitals,
and once again use their traditional puppet-making skills to
build yet another extravagant Bush effigy to burn in protest.
Although Bush's inept management of the U.S. credit market
has dragged down the entire world economy, Bush always kept
the international markets in papier-mâché, cardboard, glue,
craft paint, lighter fluid, and matches humming right along.

President Bush set the all-time record for the most people worldwide to simultaneously take to the streets to protest
him. On February 15, 2003, approximately 15 million people

in roughly 800 cities across the world marched against Bush's imminent invasion of Iraq. This massive display against Bush shattered the record for protest against any one person in the history of humanity, a species that has thrown up a fair amount of individuals to complain about. We're number one! We're number one! We're number . . . hey, where did all the foreign tourists go?

Most Americans didn't bother to renew their international passport for travel once Bush came into office. The few

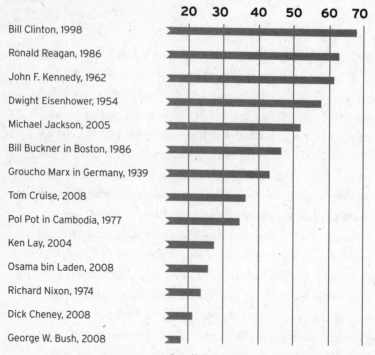

Approval Ratings Comparison
Selected approval ratings, in percentages

	20	30	40	50	60	70
Bill Clinton, 1998						
Ronald Reagan, 1986						
John F. Kennedy, 1962						
Dwight Eisenhower, 1954						
Michael Jackson, 2005						
Bill Buckner in Boston, 1986						
Groucho Marx in Germany, 1939						
Tom Cruise, 2008						
Pol Pot in Cambodia, 1977						
Ken Lay, 2004						
Osama bin Laden, 2008						
Richard Nixon, 1974						
Dick Cheney, 2008						
George W. Bush, 2008						

Source: Stanford University's *2008 Statistical Abstract of Who's Hot, Who's Not*

who did made sure to buy Canadian-flag patches to sew onto their backpacks as a disguise. Remember the days when you could travel abroad without feeling ashamed about your government? Perhaps the American fear of being chased through the cobblestone streets of foreign cities by angry mobs just for being an American was a contributing factor to the demise of so many airlines. Bush is the very first U.S. president in history to have a solid majority of Europeans (including an astonishing 77 percent of Germans) view his presidency as the biggest threat to world peace and stability. Out of anyone, the Germans would be the ones to know about the dangers of trying to control the world through unilateral military force. If you did find the courage to travel while American, it was hard to miss how militarized our U.S. embassies in foreign capitals have become. Of course there's the threat of terrorism to protect against, but it's obvious that all of the Marines, attack dogs, and concrete blast walls at our embassies were put in place as protection against the pissed-off-at-us locals, as well as any al-Qaeda fighters who might parachute in from Waziristan.

The antipathy of the world against Bush, as well as Bush's against the world, is glaringly obvious when he traveled abroad. George shut down whole cities when he came to visit, turning them into armed camps. His motorcade of black, bulletproof SUVs rolled in like Bush was a conquering general. Surface-to-air missile batteries were placed around his hotel. Roads, trains, and waterways were shut down. No-fly zones were put into effect, except for police helicopters overhead. Police snipers were posted on rooftops. Foreign governments spent millions of dollars on riot police, rubber bullets, teargas, water cannons, and armored vehicles to lock down the anti-Bush crowd, just for the pleasure of Bush dropping by. Way to spread that freedom, George. When Bush traveled to Genoa, Italy, in 2001, he didn't even stay in the beautiful, historic city, but on a luxury cruise liner anchored offshore, patrolled by armed guards and dogs. Bush and his neoconservative henchmen often said that many people around the world are inherently anti-American, because they hate us for our freedoms or are jealous of our prosperity. I don't think a majority of people around the world hate average Americans, George. They just really hate you.

Bush's bullheaded rush into war, along with his general frat-boy douchebagginess, alienated our nation's traditional allies. A perfect moment that captured Bush's disagreeable personality was at a G8 Summit meeting, when Bush decided to sneak up behind the Prime Minister of Germany, Angela Merkel, and give her an unrequested shoulder massage. Merkel reacted with revulsion to Bush's wandering hands, hunching up her shoulders in the universal message understood by all males over the age of fifteen: "Don't try the old back-rub trick with me!" Why would Bush target Merkel for a rubdown? The first rule of international relations is, don't go after the frosty German chick.

"The problem with the French is that they don't have a word for 'entrepreneur.' "

—George W. Bush, 2002 G8 Summit, July 9, 2002

"Do you have blacks, too?"

—George W. Bush, to Fernando Henrique Cardoso, the president of Brazil, November 2001

The North Korean Foreign Ministry once described Bush as a "a man bereft of elementary reason" and "a politically backward child." For once, the hyperbole of the Hermit Kingdom was right on the money. Bush was an embarrassment to all Americans whenever he stumbled onto the international stage. He always butchered the pronunciation of the names of foreign leaders (if he knew them in the first place) except for that one English chap, Tony Bliar—er, Blair. His complete ignorance of the world was stunning. While speaking in Australia on September 8, 2007, Bush congratulated the Australian Prime Minister for visiting his Austrian troops in Iraq. He's not even on the right continent. Here's another head-spinning quote by Bush that he vomited up in Japan: "My trip to Asia begins here in Japan for an important reason. It begins here because for a century and a half now, America and Japan have formed one of the great and enduring alliances of modern times. From that alliance has come an era of peace in the Pacific." Presumably Bush's Japanese audience thought, "Yeah, except for that war when you nuked us, you dick." Of course, Bush is only following the example that his father set in 1992, when he barfed all over Prime Minister Miyazawa's lap during a state dinner in Japan. (That moment really captured how the Bush family operates. They don't care to puke on their own lap, or into a napkin, or just on the floor, but rather all over the guy sitting next to them.) It's actually surprising that more bodily fluids haven't spontaneously erupted out of George W. Bush during international summits. Then again, Dubya doesn't travel in international circles as much as his father did. Instead of barfing on foreign heads-of-state, George prefers to choke on pretzels in the privacy of his own home.

In a humorous aside from the Israel-Palestine conflict,

A Presidential Embarrassment

What are some of George W. Bush's most infamous gaffes on the public stage?

June 14, 2006

At a White House press conference, Bush asks *Los Angeles Times* reporter Peter Wallsten, who is legally blind, "Peter, you gonna ask that question with shades on?"

November 20, 2005

Bush tugs frantically on the handle of a locked door in an effort to quickly get offstage after a speech in China.

July 18, 2006

Unaware that a nearby microphone is on, Bush talks with UK Prime Minister Tony Blair at a G8 Conference luncheon. "Yo, Blair . . . What they need to do is get Syria, to get Hezbollah to stop doing this shit . . ." says Bush through a mouthful of bread.

May 8, 2007

Bush welcomes Queen Elizabeth II to the White House. "You helped our nation celebrate its bicentennial in 177 . . . uh, in 1976," says Bush, unwittingly revealing the fact that the Queen is a 262-year-old, shape-shifting, reptilian humanoid whose longevity is attained by drinking the blood of children.

October 8, 2004

Bush mocks opponent John Kerry during a presidential debate by unbuttoning his shirt, placing his hand beneath his armpit, and producing farting sounds while Kerry is speaking.

June 3, 2004

During a state visit by Afghanistan President Hamid Karzai, Bush punches Karzai in the face for flirting with his daughter Jenna. After knocking Karzai to the floor, Bush kicks him repeatedly in the ribs.

August 8, 2008

During the opening ceremony of the Beijing Olympics, news cameras cut to Bush, who is sitting in the stands. When Bush sees himself on a large stadium screen, he laughs, places his fingertips at the corners of his eyes, and pulls his skin backward, making his eyes appear to be narrow slits.

March 14, 2007

George Bush, holding his pet Scottish terrier Barney, disembarks *Air Force One* at Ronald Reagan Washington National Airport. While waving to assembled news media, Bush clumsily drops his dog. Barney scurries away from Bush, who gives chase. When Barney makes an unexpected move, Bush accidentally steps on Barney's head and crushes his skull, killing the dog instantly.

September 3, 2008

Bush appears on a large screen via satellite to address the Republican National Convention in Saint Paul, Minnesota, ensuring his party's defeat in the 2008 presidential elections.

consider Bush's policy of "disengagement," which created the most hostile Israeli-Palestinian relations in thirty years. Wow. With his incredible ability to engender personal hatred for himself, Bush somehow unified the Israelis and Palestinians on at least one issue.

One country that is desperate enough to still pretend to like Bush is Albania, where he was received by enthusiastic crowds on June 12, 2007. Of course, Bush's warm reception there can be explained by Albania's hope that in return for their best truck driver that they sent to Iraq, Bush will give them enough money to buy that second goat they have their eye on. The high point of the trip, and a moment that shows this relationship perfectly, was when Bush was shaking hands with an excited, milling crowd of Albanians and got his watch stolen right off his wrist by some sticky-fingered local. Three basic rules for international travel, George: don't drink the water in Mexico, don't eat the food in England, and don't wear a wristwatch in Albania. You really should get out more.

It was obvious how far America's world reputation has nosedived when you look at the nations that Bush managed to cobble together for his "Coalition of the Willing" to illegally invade Iraq. These were primarily small, poor countries that gladly grabbed Bush's offer of foreign aid cash in return for making Bush look a little less insane. The impoverished Eastern European countries of Bulgaria, Hungary, and Romania were just happy to do something to make a little money besides another porno film. The remote Pacific island nations of Micronesia, Tonga, and the Marshall Islands joined when Bush promised to send them a rescue ship—staffed by a capable skipper, his first mate, a brilliant scientist, a Hollywood film starlet, a lovable down-home gal, and a wealthy New England couple—who would get them the hell off of Micronesia, Tonga, and the Marshall Islands. Mongolia signed up when Bush promised that he would help their hordes to pillage and conquer all of Eurasia once again under the glory of a new Great Khanate. Rwanda leapt into action when Bush told them that there were a heck of a lot of Tutsis in Iraq. Japan joined the coalition just to be polite. Even with forty-nine countries on Bush's veneer-of-legitimacy coalition list, 99 percent of the troops in Iraq are American and British. There remains only a wee squad of 4,000 British soldiers in Iraq, compared with the 144,000 American troops. No, I didn't forget Poland. They pulled out their 900 Poles when they lamely excused themselves to Bush by saying they were just traditionally more comfortable being invaded than doing the invading.

When Russia put Georgia in a headlock and started squeezing after Georgia had attacked South Ossetia in August 2008, Bush was outraged. He actually proclaimed that "bullying and intimidation are not acceptable ways to conduct foreign policy in the twenty-first century." You know, George, that argument doesn't hold much weight anymore, thanks to you. Bullying and intimidation are the central tenets of your own Bush Doctrine, although the tough talk usually escalates to bombing and military occupation. Savor the absurd grandiosity of that term—*The Bush Doctrine*—as if it will be printed in history textbooks next to that Monroe guy. The teacher will ask, "Class, what can you tell me about the Bush Doctrine?" and the kid with the glasses will stand up, salute, and say, "The Bush Doctrine gives the right to the president to attack and replace the government of any country he wants if he thinks that country is looking at us funny." Very good, gold star. The

Bush record of unwarranted, preemptive, let's-get-'em-before-they-get-us attacks have emboldened repressive governments everywhere to launch brutal offensives against ethnic minorities and political rivals. Bush advanced the use of violence and defeated the efforts of diplomacy around the world.

To understate massively, with Bush in charge, Earth has become a much more tense and twitchy place. Of course, the nations of the world have been wary of the 900-pound gorilla that is the United States since the fall of the Soviet Union. But Bush decided to throw open the cage of that gorilla, which ran out in a berserker rage and jumped up and down on a lot of people. Seeing what this hairy beast could do, it came as no surprise that the countries who hadn't been invaded yet by Bush decided to beef up their defense capability. Russian military expenditures have tripled during the Bush years. China is transforming its military into a high-tech force capable of projecting power globally by 2010, and have replaced their land-based nuclear arsenal of twenty intercontinental ballistic missiles from the 1970s with sixty new multiple-warhead missiles capable of reaching the United States. North Korea, with the fire of being on Bush's "Axis of Evil" lit under their ass, managed to bang out some nukes even though they haven't eaten in months. They didn't want to end up like Iraq, and building a nuclear weapon was the best way to avoid that fate. Bush's bluster and belligerence have not made the world safer, but much more dangerous. He has not achieved peace among nations, but rather suspicion, paranoia, and the stockpiling of weapons.

Bill Clinton may have stained a dress, but Bush's stain on our national reputation is infinitely larger, darker, and greasier. The stain of Bush will also be much more difficult

We Don't Sign No Stinkin' Treaties

In response to numerous international agreements to address world issues, Bush has repeatedly told the planet that it can shove its treaties up its South Pole. Here are the treaties, the problems they attempt to solve, and Bush's preferred special-interest groups that swayed him to vote no.

Treaty	Problem	Bush's Interest Group
UN Human Rights Commission resolution making AIDS drugs affordable	Possible extinction of human life in Africa	Pharmaceutical corporations
UN Human Rights Commission resolution to recognize food as a basic human right	World hunger	Famine, Bush's favorite horseman of the apocalypse
International Criminal Court Treaty	War crime	War criminals
Ottawa Treaty	Landmines scattered across the planet	The actual landmines – Bush loves each and every one of them
Kyoto Protocol	Global warming	Reptiles
Organisation for Economic Cooperation and Development talks	Off-shore tax and money-laundering havens	Tax evaders and drug lords
World Conference Against Racism	Racism	Ku Klux Klan
International Plan for Cleaner Energy	Planet-fouling pollution	General Motors, Exxon, Saudi Arabian royal family
UN resolution to end embargo of Cuba	Starving Cuban grandmothers	Rich Cubans in Florida who want their golf courses back
International Court of Justice ruling on U.S. crimes in Nicaragua	Covert warfare against civilian populations	Death squads
International Conference for a Global Ban on Anti-Personnel Landmines	Indiscriminate air bombing	John McCain
UN Convention on the Elimination of All Forms of Discrimination against Women	Sexism	Bros before hoes
UN Convention on the Rights of the Child	Exploitation of children	Child-haters

to get out. Bush is the first president in our history to see the United Nations remove the United States from its Human Rights Commission, what with Bush's international network of torture camps and all. He is also the first president to force the United Nations to remove the United States from its elections monitoring board, after George made a mockery of representative democracy in his rise to power. A bit miffed over this snub, Bush refused United Nations election inspectors during the 2002 U.S. elections. Isn't that what countries like Zimbabwe do? Bush withdrew the United States from the International Criminal Court and the International Court of Justice, possibly forcing aggrieved parties to address their grievances at the hands of the United States by setting bombs instead of filing papers. He even refused to allow international inspectors access to U.S.-held prisoners of war, and by default our country no longer abides by the Geneva Conventions. One of the American freedoms that Bush worked so hard to achieve is the freedom to commit war crimes.

The real rub of all this is that it didn't have to be this way. The worldwide outpouring of grief and sympathy for the United States after 9/11 was tremendous. Anyone, no matter where they lived, could sympathize with normal people on their way to work being crushed and incinerated. The fact that the majority of the carnage happened in the international, multicultural city of New York only added to the planet's compassion for us. We could have coasted on sympathy hugs for years. On September 12, 2001, you could have dropped into any café in Baghdad, of all places, and been treated like a king. "Special price for you, my friend," the shopkeeper would say, smiling warmly beneath his thick mustache. "A nice cup of mint tea, on the house. And let me fix you a plate of our delicious house special, lamb shawarma, free of charge. Also, we didn't do it." Yet Bush squandered the goodwill of the world, making the United States the most resented country on the planet—possibly the grandest diplomatic failure in world history. Our president acted like a bully in the schoolyard, and after a while, none of the other children wanted to hang out with us. Except for that fat Polish kid, who Bush would give lunch money to beat up on the Arabs for him.

Why does all of this matter? Who cares what the world thinks of us? as some conservative who thrives on being hated and has no desire to ever leave Tulsa, Oklahoma, might ask. If no one respects us, and in fact resents and fears us, no one will cooperate with us and no one will help us. We won't get the courtesy of a "heads-up" when something terrible is headed our way. Just one example will do it—we need the help of other countries to stop the proliferation of nuclear weapons around the globe. Treating other nations with respect is essential to our national security, our economy, and the health of our shared natural environment. And who knows—with the way that the economy is going, one day we might be grateful for offers of Cuban doctors and Venezuelan heating oil. You get back what you put out there. As the golden rule of all the world's major religions states, do onto others as you would wish them to do onto you. (Bush didn't do very well in Sunday school, either.) Once upon a time, we could positively influence other countries through the democratic ideals expressed in our Constitution. Bush threw away all that. That's what happens when your president invades a country, for no solid reason, after everyone pleads with him not to. And also talks with his mouth full of food in front of shocked Europeans with very good table manners.

The last, humiliating reminder of how far our international status has fallen under Bush happened during the opening ceremonies of the Beijing Summer Olympics. The Chinese stuck Bush way up in the nosebleed row of the stadium, seated between the school board chairman of Ho Chi Minh City and the deputy mayor of Siem Reap. The president of the United States had to use binoculars to see the ceremony. Even though they tried to put Bush as far out of the spotlight as possible, Bush still managed to make himself look like a jackass: pulling goofy faces, stumbling to his seat and having to be supported by Secret Service agents, holding up an American flag backward, and then slapping a smaller American flag on a stick impatiently against his leg. He looked like he just wanted to get the hell out of there and go back home. Now you've got that chance, George. The world won't miss you.

STUFF IT IN THE MEMORY HOLE

We'll Never Know His Darkest Secrets

How many skeletons are in George W. Bush's closet? As in, actual skeletons? The hysterical paranoia that bubbles out of the ground when a Bush is running the country is understandable. Their overt actions are so brutal and terrifying, you have to wonder how bad their covert ones are.

Our previous Bush president, George H.W. Bush, joined his first secret society when he was eight years old, at Andover prep school. He did not tell his son the truth about Santa Claus until Dubya was thirty-four. Yet George W. Bush took this betrayal as a master lesson in deceitfulness and has protected his family's secrets throughout his career. George Junior actually called himself his father's "loyalty enforcer" during the 1988 and 1992 presidential campaigns, and drilled everyone on his "grenade" rule—if there was a grenade coming at his father, they had to jump on it. Soon after he was appointed president in 2001, George signed Executive Order 13233, sealing off Ronald

Reagan's and his father's presidential records, which were about to be released. Researchers and the public may never be allowed to see them. Loose lips sink pirate ships, after all.

"I am mindful not only of preserving executive powers for myself, but for predecessors as well."

—George W. Bush, January 29, 2001

"If the people were to ever find out what we have done, we would be chased down the streets and lynched."

—George H.W. Bush, in an interview with Sarah McClendon, White House correspondent from 1944 to 2001, printed in McClendon's newsletter, June 1992

The code of *omerta* runs strong in the Bush crime family, from generation to generation. It's necessary to cover up their traitorous history of secretly aiding our national enemies in order to profit from war; along with the coups, both covert and overt, that seek to undermine or even replace the U.S. government. Prescott Bush, the grandfather of our current Bush-spawn, was in business with Nazi Germany throughout the 1930s and early 1940s. He was one of the key financiers who coordinated the flow of investments from American multi-millionaires into Nazi Germany. Even after the United States had entered the war in 1941, Prescott Bush worked for and profited from companies closely involved with the German industrial titans who financed Adolf Hitler's rise to power. The U.S. government eventually seized the assets of four banks and businesses in which Prescott Bush was a director or shareholder, under the Trading with the Enemy Act.

Prescott's Nazi front operations, which established the Bush family fortune and set up its political dynasty, did the bidding of the German companies that built the Nazi war machine and used slave labor at Auschwitz.

If that weren't enough, Senator Prescott Bush was a leader of "The Business Plot," an attempted fascist takeover against President Franklin Delano Roosevelt in 1933. Prescott Bush, with his fellow cabal of right-wing politicians, industrialists, and financiers, secretly approached Marine Corps Major Gen. Smedley Butler with a plan to lead a 500,000-strong rogue army of veterans to assassinate FDR and end the New Deal that threatened their business interests. General Butler worked with this shock-and-awe fascist putsch just long enough to identify who was behind it, then testified to Congress on who the traitors were. This is not a flight of fancy; it's all in the *Congressional Record*. If it weren't for General Butler, a two-time Medal of Honor winner and the author of the 1935 antiwar classic *War Is a Racket,* we could have had an unbroken string of Bushes as our maximum leaders since 1933.

Prescott's son, George H.W. Bush, continued the family tradition of undermining the U.S. government by running the shadowy Iran-Contra affair in the 1980s. (The overt power-grab opportunity that the Reagan assassination attempt provided, committed by the son of one of Bush's closest Texas oil supporters, did not come to fruition.) During an official U.S.-decreed embargo on arms sales to Ayatollah Khomeini's Iran, George H.W. Bush was secretly selling weapons to Iran, then sent that money to right-wing Contra death squads in Nicaragua to wage war on nuns, labor leaders, poor workers, and that country's democratically elected government. Both of these actions were expressly forbidden by U.S. law. While Ronald Reagan napped through the 1980s, our real leader, former CIA director and President-of-Vice Bush, also supported CIA asset Osama bin Laden and equipped and trained the men who would become al-Qaeda and the Taliban, back when he called them "freedom fighters" and not "terrorists." Afghan fighters were so heroic back in 1988, when they were shooting Russians and not us, that they could co-star with Sylvester Stallone in *Rambo III,* blowing up the bad guys together. George H.W. Bush also sent biological and chemical weapons to Saddam Hussein's Iraq, so that George W. Bush could also invade that country on the false charges that they still had all of the weapons that his father had given them twenty years ago.

As for the enemy in the headlines today, it is no surprise that the bin Laden and Bush families are business partners, as reported in the *Wall Street Journal Europe* on September 28, 2001: "Bin Laden Family Has Intricate Ties with Washington: Saudi Clan Has Had Access to Influential Republicans." The first sentence says it all: "If the U.S. boosts defense spending in its quest to stop Osama bin Laden's alleged terrorist activities, there may be one unexpected beneficiary: Mr. bin Laden's family." The only questionable word in that sentence is "unexpected." The bin Laden family owns the Saudi Binladin Group, a huge construction company that made billions of dollars building U.S. military bases in Saudi Arabia in the 1980s, as well as their son Osama's CIA-financed cave complexes in Afghanistan. After Osama bin Laden was accused of the 1996 Khobar Towers bombing in Saudi Arabia that killed nineteen U.S. servicemen, Saudi Binladin Group got another lucrative contract to build higher-security military barracks and airfields for U.S. troops. The bin Laden family has publicly disowned Osama and his terrorist attacks, but this black sheep certainly brings in a lot of cash for the family business. Until October of 2001, the bin Ladens were an investor in the Carlyle Group, the world's largest private equity investment firm, based in Washington, D.C., and centered on the war industry. Our former president George H.W. Bush worked for the Carlyle Group from 1998 to 2003, and has made the pilgrimage to the bin Laden family's headquarters in Saudi Arabia, where he was presumably patted on the head for helping to net the bin Laden family a 40 percent annualized rate of return on their Carlyle investments. On September 10, 2001, George H.W. Bush sat down with Osama's half-brother and Carlyle guest of honor Shafig bin Laden, to discuss the joint interests of the Saudi Binladin Group and the Carlyle Group. After 9/11, these two groups mutually severed financial ties, but not out of any sense of guilt or shame over the gross conflicts-of-interest at stake. Instead, a Carlyle executive told the *Wall Street Journal,* "I don't want to spend my life talking to reporters."

To start his first Texas energy company in 1977, George W. Bush went into business with Osama bin Laden's half-brother, Salem, who actively lobbied for donations to his half-bro's organization as late as 1988. (Salem bin Laden died in a freak accident aboard a tiny, ultralight aircraft that year, when he strangely flew right into high-voltage power lines next to a flying field in San Antonio, Texas.) The United States ignored several offers from Sudan to extradite Osama bin Laden to the United States, even after the U.S. embassy bombings in Africa (yes, we can include Bill Clinton as a member of the Bush crime family). President Bush ordered the FBI to "back off" on investigating the bin Laden family soon after taking office. This included Osama's son, Abdullah bin Laden, who was under investigation by U.S. agents for his links to the Saudi-funded World

Association of Muslim Youth, accused by both Pakistan and India as a supporter of terrorism. After 9/11, many bin Laden family members were quickly flown out of the United States. Bush knowingly allowed Osama bin Laden and the elite of al-Qaeda to escape Afghanistan into the hinterlands of Pakistan, and now that's where our next war will take place, as promised by our new president of hope and change, Barack Obama.

So what exactly is going on here—besides the rational judgment that the mysterious Saudi millionaire Osama bin Laden is an asset of the Bush-led military-industrial complex, who is protected and positioned in whichever country the United States wants to invade next? We'll never know exactly how all of these facts fit together, since twenty-seven key pages in the *9/11 Commission Report,* nearly the entire chapter dealing with the Saudi Arabian government's connections to the hijackers, was blacked out by George W. Bush. The 9/11 attacks were immediately pinned on Osama bin Laden (even though no less than Dick Cheney and the FBI now tell us, as noted earlier, that they have no legal proof on that), providing the flimsy excuse for the Afghanistan and Iraq wars, which killed hundreds of thousands more and massively enriched Bush's inner circle yet again. It makes your head spin to consider that we have been fighting this War on Terror for seven years, and the initial reason for starting the war has most likely been dead by kidney failure for six years now. Osama bin Laden had advanced diabetes and needed professional treatment from a large dialysis machine several times a week to stay alive. The caves of Waziristan are not known for their electricity, clean water, sterile settings, and readily available kidney specialist doctors and dialysis technicians.

The driving force of Bush's presidency, the 9/11 attacks,

remain shrouded in secrecy. The FBI seized surveillance video-tapes from the hotel and gas station across the road from the Pentagon immediately after the attack and have never released the footage. In 2002, five still frames from a Pentagon surveillance video were released that did not show a 757 crashing into the Pentagon. Six air traffic controllers who told of their communications with the hijacked planes were tape-recorded later in the day on September 11, 2001. That tape was destroyed by Federal Aviation Administration managers, as reported on May 6, 2004, in the *Washington Post*. The black boxes of the two planes that hit the World Trade Center were claimed to have never been found, even though a New York firefighter and a 9/11 rescue worker publicly stated that they had found three of the four boxes and handed them over to the FBI. An unnamed source at the National Transportation Safety Board says that the government did retrieve the boxes. Their cockpit voice recorders and flight data have never been released. The wreckage of Ground Zero was hastily collected and shipped off to smelting furnaces and dumps, disabling any scientific efforts to understand the unprecedented engineering failure of the World Trade Towers. At the Pentagon, military personnel were out on the lawn immediately after the attack, picking up pieces of debris and carting them away. Bush did everything he could to suppress an investigation of 9/11, until the demand from victims' families became overwhelming. Once the 9/11 Commission was under way, Bush resisted funding it, opposed time extensions, denied requests for documents, and tried to stop National Security Advisor Condoleezza Rice from testifying. When Bush finally agreed to have his own hush-hush "conversation" with the 9–11 commissioners, he said that it had to be private, not under oath, not recorded, limited to one hour, and Cheney had to be there to hold his hand.

George H.W. Bush really let his hair down in the Sarah McClendon interview in 1992, when he explained what Iran-Contra was all about: "The continuous consolidation of money and power into higher, tighter, and righter hands." Throughout their history, the Bush family has picked out, supported, assisted, protected, and manipulated truly horrible international villains in order to enrich themselves at the cost of millions of human lives, when they're not orchestrating overtly fascist power grabs to take over and loot the United States government. You can see why they like to keep their real agenda secret, preferring to bedazzle the public with nonsense like "we're spreadin' freedom" or "the illumination of a thousand points of light." If we are the points of light, the Bush family is the blackness of the galactic void, secret and unknowable, surrounding all of us scattered, twinkling stars. Their expanding darkness presses in and consumes us, until we flicker and wink out.

George W. Bush made it a priority to expand that darkness. In 2003 alone, Bush spent $6.5 billion to create fourteen million new classified documents and secure old secrets—the highest level of secrecy spending in ten years. Bush spent $120 classifying documents for every $1 he spent declassifying documents. Federal spending on paper shredding increased more than 600 percent since Bush took office. The Bush administration—reversing years of bipartisan tradition—refused to answer requests from Democratic members of Congress about how the White House spent taxpayer money. The classified "black" budget of the Department of Defense, the spending they provide no information on, nearly doubled in the Bush years, up to $32 billion. The Bush administration spent millions of dollars and defied numerous court orders in an effort to conceal from the public who exactly participated in Dick Cheney's 2001 energy task force. As for Cheney's connections to his "former" employer Halliburton, which is holding Dick's deferred yearly salary and stock options for him, his open and honest response to Senator Patrick Leahy's questioning was "Go fuck yourself."

Reporters who might shine some light into this dark hole of secrecy had a tough time under Bush. He corrupted PBS by appointing a right-wing enforcer to shut down investigative reporting on the Bush regime. He spent hundreds of millions to produce fake "video news segments" of pro-Bush propaganda, aired nationwide as real news, featuring Americans "thanking" George. He paid off pundits under the table to sing his praises. He pushed with the most powerful broadcast corporations to bring about monopoly control on information. He clamped

Bush's Secrecy Budget, 2008

Federal yearly expenditures allotted for the destruction of sensitive information climbed from $452,807 in 2000 to over $3.5 million in 2008. How did Bush spend the money?

Thick black markers $464,459

Shredding $776,912

Incinerating $529,504

Burying $438,387

Scattering at sea $332,751

Gobbling $585,776

Herd of man-eating pigs $368,923

Source: None of your goddamn business

down on the Freedom of Information Act, refusing to release the most basic requests for federal data. Reporters in Iraq had to be embedded with U.S. troops, skewing our perception of the war. Basic facts like civilian casualty counts, images of U.S. flag–draped coffins, or the worst of the Abu Ghraib torture photos were secretly stuffed into a dark hole by Bush. He held the fewest number of press conferences of any modern president and made a mockery of them by steering tough questions to his planted reporter/gay prostitute Jeff Gannon.

What dark, shadowy holes do these people crawl out of? The Tomb of the ultrasecret fraternity Skull and Bones at Yale University is one of them. Prescott, George H.W., and little George are all Bonesmen. As for the six billion of us who aren't lucky enough to be one of the fifteen Yalies tapped each year to join this occult coven, they call us "barbarians." Prescott Bush pulled off the legendary grave-robbing of what he believed to be the Apache chief Geronimo's skull in 1918 to display with pride in the Bonesmen's Tomb (robbing treasures from "the barbarians" is a time-honored Skull and Bones tradition). The Bonesmen still like to kiss the skull in their rituals. I wish this was a joke, but George H.W. Bush actually took the secret nickname of Magog, the biblical demon who brings about the Apocalypse, which is reserved for the Bonesman with the most sexual experience (*eww*). From the ledge of a nearby building in 2001, Rob Rosenbaum of the *New York Observer* used night-vision cameras to film in an inner courtyard the initiation ceremony of this 176-year-old hidden cult, and it is as weird and sadistic as you can imagine it to be.

In 2004, when both Bush and John Kerry (his S&B nickname is Long Devil) were asked by Tim Russert on *Meet the Press* about their membership in Skull and Bones, they had the exact same response: "It's so secret, I can't talk about it [creepy laugh]." Enjoy your free and open election, America. Your two choices for president both went to the most elite university in the country, then joined within two years of each other a fifteen-member secret society composed of the elite of that elite—the ultimate old boys' network of roughly eight hundred living members that has included presidents, senators, Supreme Court chief justices, and leaders throughout the business, finance, media, military, and intelligence fields. They've been going strong since 1832.

Back around 1910, when she was a young girl growing up in Washington, D.C., my grandmother was actually struck by the automobile of President Taft, our other Skull and Bones president besides Gog and Magog Bush. Reportedly Taft stuck his fat head out of the window and asked, "Is the little girl all right?" My grandmother's bicycle was put in the car's trunk and she was driven home. So perhaps I should be thankful that my grandmother was not sent off to a Skull and Bones–run child slavery ring. Who knows how I would have turned out? Thanks, Taft.

These strange and secretive men enjoy frolicking out in the fresh air as well. Several hundred of the most powerful men in the world gather every summer, as they have since 1872, at the remote 2,700 acres of the Bohemian Grove in the redwood forests of Northern California. George W. Bush and his father have attended this all-male bacchanalia many times. Their patron saint is John of Nepomuk, who legend says suffered death at the hands of a Bohemian monarch rather than disclose the secrets of his queen. A large wooden carving of Saint John, with his index finger over his lips, stands at the shore of the lake in Bohemian Grove, idolizing the secrecy kept

Above Top Secret

The Bush administration's obsession with secrecy has left us with many questions, but no answers. What are the most tantalizing mysteries that Bush has made certain to bury for all time?

1 Is FEMA building large-scale concentration camps in isolated rural areas across the country, and if so, why? (*Note: This issue may actually clear up before too long.*)

2 Why do only Democratic politicians die in mysterious small-plane crashes?

3 Did Bush engage in dad-sourced insider trading when he sold his stock in Harken Energy, earning $1 million, just a few weeks before Iraq invaded Kuwait in 1990?

4 What in the world could Dick Cheney and officials from Exxon-Mobil, Conoco, and Royal Dutch Shell have been discussing while poring over maps of Iraq's oil fields in secret energy policy meetings in early 2001? (*This one's a real puzzler.*)

5 Why did Bush make sure that anyone with the last name of bin Laden get a quick flight out of the United States, no questions asked, immediately after 9/11?

6 Was photo editor Bob Stevens at American Media Inc. in Boca Raton, Florida, the first fatality of the 2001 anthrax attacks, murdered because he had scandalous photos of George W. Bush and John Kerry cavorting naked in a coffin during a Skull and Bones secret society initiation ritual?

7 Why was Rudy Giuliani's company Bio One, which specializes in anthrax decontamination, contracted to "clean up" the American Media Inc. building, including its photo library?

8 What was George W. Bush's father's personal schedule in Dallas, Texas, on November 22, 1963?

9. Did Hunter S. Thompson, who was working on an article at the time of his death in 2005 that featured what he felt was hard evidence that the World Trade Towers were brought down by controlled demolition, and who expressed fears for his own safety to journalist Paul William Roberts of the Toronto *Globe and Mail* the night before his death, saying "They're gonna make it look like suicide—I know how these bastards think," really shoot himself while asking his wife on the phone to come home from the gym and help him with his writing?

10. Why did George Bush Sr. sit down with Shafig bin Laden, Osama's brother, at a Carlyle Group meeting on the morning of September 11, 2001, and what exactly did they have for breakfast?

by the Grove's attendees throughout its history. Hundreds of prostitutes, both male and female, flock to the area every summer to service our nation's leaders. Luckily, undercover reporters have infiltrated and videotaped this secret society as well. The highlight of Bohemian Grove is the "Cremation of Care" ceremony, where a human effigy representing the "dull cares" of the human conscience is burned by hooded priests with torches at the foot of a 45-foot-high owl statue. A recording of human screams is played at high volume from hidden speakers. You can watch video of this ceremony online. Then everyone gets wasted and runs around in the woods wearing women's wigs and fake tits.

Who knows what all of this occult symbolism adds up to? The undeniable facts are that George W. Bush and his inner circle revel in secret, hidden rituals of sadism and death, and the rest of us are definitely not invited. We have already examined Bush's reverse speech disorder, but this coded, bipolar language emits from a deeply reversed personality as well. Bush's surface personality that was presented to us was that he was squeaky clean—a bar of strong Texas soap that could scrub out the stains that Bill Clinton had sprayed across the White House drapes. However, his real personality underneath this wholesome crust was rotten to the core. The trusted and prestigious Bush family pedigree meant that George grew up torturing frogs as a child. This levelheaded conservative was a cocaine-snorting, alcoholic, drunk-driving, service-avoiding, company-bankrupting fuck-up. This devoted Christian frolicked in the bizarre rituals of his Skull and Bones cult and attended a mock human sacrifice to a pagan totem in the dark forests of Bohemian Grove. This compassionate conservative branded frat brothers on the buttocks with a heated coat hanger and mocked a woman he had executed as governor of Texas, pursing his lips together and saying in a squeaky, pleading voice, "Please don't kill me." This careful economic steward spent like a drunken wastrel, pointlessly pouring money out of the nation in thundering, fraudulent waterfalls of lost wealth. This true patriot's real goal for the country was to loot its treasure from the "barbarians" into higher, tighter, and righter hands. What was served up as warm, delicious, good old American apple pie was in fact something very different and disturbed. Given how deeply reversed Bush's real personality is from his manufactured image, you can understand his need for secrecy.

"The very word 'secrecy' is repugnant in a free and
open society; and we are as a people inherently and
historically opposed to secret societies, to secret oaths,
and to secret proceedings."

—John F. Kennedy, April 27, 1961

"I'll be long gone before some smart person ever figures
out what happened inside this Oval Office."

—George W. Bush, May 12, 2008

Conclusion

ANYBODY GOT SOME CHANGE?

George W. Bush has given us so many memories, but it would be unforgivable to leave out the one moment in time that made all of these other memories possible. This would be the day that led to the Afghanistan War, the Iraq War, the PATRIOT Act, the Department of Der Vaterland Security, a paradise of virgins for suicide bombers, the torture at Guantánamo Bay and Abu Ghraib, government spying on Americans, illegal imprisonment, anthrax in our mailboxes, depleted uranium, WMD, Osama bin Laden's videotapes, Halliburton no-bid contracts, IEDs, Predator drones, the siege of Fallujah, hidden U.S. soldiers' coffins, the beheadings of Daniel Pearl and Nick Berg, the 20th hijacker Zacarias Moussaoui, the shoe-bomber Richard Reid, the dirty-bomber José Padilla, Khalid Sheikh Mohammed, Abu Zarqawi, Muqtada al-Sadr, the Mahdi Army, 3/11 in Madrid, 7/7 in London, our Orange Alerts and air travel toiletries miniaturized inside Ziploc bags, this entire alien universe of jagged terror and death that we woke up to over seven years ago.

Where would we be without 9/11?

It was the most surreal, frightening day of the entire Bush era. For several weeks after 9/11 in New York City, the standard question when you greeted people was "Are you okay?" The real meaning of this was "Did anyone close to you die?" The lawyer who vetted my questions about 9/11 in the book *Citizen You!* lost a friend at the World Trade Center. People who ask questions about 9/11 care about 9/11. Instead, within hours of the attack, Osama bin Laden was definitively pinned for this "completely unexpected" crime, and Bush invaded Afghanistan to catch him in a war that the U.S. military had already planned and mobilized for. Bush didn't bother catching Osama when he had the chance, and the official explanations for 9/11 didn't hold up, as admitted by the FBI. The real evidence of the 9/11 crime scenes was seized, suppressed, or destroyed by the Bush administration, which is a crime in itself. The 9/11 Commission was stifled at every step by the White House, and we are left with no real answers. I want nothing more than to see the men who committed 9/11 be brought to justice in a real criminal investigation, which doesn't involve torture-produced fake confessions. Instead, Bush gave us the fully militarized Global War on Terror, invading two defenseless countries and killing hundreds of thousands of people who had nothing to do with the 9/11 attacks.

A military response to terrorism doesn't work because it plays right into Osama bin Laden's hands. Or was it George W. Bush's? It's easy to get confused, because none of it makes any sense. Our military attacks and torture inflict harm and humiliation on civilian populations, encouraging more to volunteer for al-Qaeda. Increased terror attacks lead to escalated military action by the United States, and the cycle of pain continues. This is the script of al-Qaeda, not the United States. They want the cultural rift of war, to draw more people to their cause. We don't have to give that to them. If we're not decapitating their mothers with 500-pound bombs, al-Qaeda will have a harder time signing up young men to take revenge as kamikaze killers. Military occupations hinder real efforts against terrorism, such as police work and undercover intelligence gathering. Full-on war only creates more terrorists and enemies of the United States. I don't think many families of 9/11 victims relish watching more random, normal people in cities around the world getting bombed and killed to honor the memory of their own lost loved ones. The Global War on Terror, in all its capitalized monstrosity, is the most counterproductive approach imaginable to effectively fight terrorism as well as a pathetic lie to justify the Pentagon maintaining its Cold War–level spending.

> **"I'm the commander—see, I don't need to explain—I do not need to explain why I say things. That's the interesting thing about being the president. Maybe somebody needs to explain to me why they say something, but I don't feel like I owe anybody an explanation."**
>
> —George W. Bush, interviewed by Bob Woodward, Crawford, Texas, August 20, 2002

Bush's response to 9/11 was the driving force to his presidency, and the consequences of his actions still hang heavy

Spencer Platt/Getty Images

The nation suffers its worst terrorist attack in history.

The Education Channel, Sarasota, FL, courtesy of
www.thememoryhole.org

Bush lets his mind stray from *The Pet Goat* to wonder how much of
the Constitution he can suspend now.

around our necks. But that was then, and this is now. We're all wondering where we go from here. Mmm, can you smell that change that the 'Rack is cooking? Here are a few bold, spicy ideas: Let's withdraw troops from Iraq and Afghanistan, sooner rather than later. Afghanistan is not called "the grave-yard of empires" for nothing. Don't worry, Obama, you don't have to prove to everyone how tough you are by escalating the war against one of the poorest countries in the world. We've all seen the photos of you with your shirt off—you're looking plenty buff, dude. Let's be really brave and declare an end to the War on Terror (al-Qaeda will be disappointed). We can put those efforts and resources into careful police work and intel-ligence gathering that actually seeks to stop terrorism, instead of promoting false terror claims to justify illogical, full-blown wars that only destabilize fragile states further. Let's stop tor-turing massive swaths of civilians and killing them in pointless bombing strikes. Besides the obvious morality of this posi-tion, it's simply a step toward self-preservation. Unleashing random violence against civilians only ensures that random violence will eventually boomerang back on us.

Let's work with the Israelis and Palestinians toward a viable two-state solution—you've been fighting each other for sixty years, guys, it's time to learn how to share. It will be difficult for both sides, but at this point, it looks like a much better option than trying to completely wipe each other out. Let's repeal the PATRIOT Act, or at least force the president to come up with a probable-cause warrant that is approved 99 percent of the time if he wants to wiretap your phone. As we save them from bankruptcy with more bailout money, let's force the Big Three automakers to build cars that meet sane fuel-efficiency standards for a change, instead of giving

Bush's Next Gig

What are the pros and cons of George W. Bush's future employment options?

Job	Pros	Cons
Small-town Texas sheriff	Has seen every episode of *Walker, Texas Ranger*	Is actually a big pussy
"Dominant master" sex worker for Republican politicians	Huge customer base	Insider leaks
International drug lord	Has all the connections; speaks Spanish	Crockett and Tubbs
Brush-clearer	His true passion	Those prickly thistles that get in your socks
Alcoholic	Years of experience	Laura
President of Paraguay	Already owns land for an estate	Can't get a good cheeseburger
Villainous professional wrestling manager	Knows how to backstab his own fighters	"Hacksaw" Jim Duggan
Swimming pool lifeguard	Can continue to keep Americans safe	Sunburn
Wal-Mart greeter	Enjoys encouraging Americans to shop	Pay sucks
Zookeeper	Animals don't talk back to you	Children throwing peanuts at him
CIA interrogator	Can still brand buttocks using a red-hot coat hanger with the best of them	Been there, done that

them incentives to build mammoth, gas-guzzling SUVs. Those Hummers became dinosaurs even quicker than we thought, didn't they? Let's stop giving most of the nation's wealth to the war industry, at the expense of social programs, infrastructure, and the environment. Let's outlaw the "exotic financial instruments" of Wall Street that our savings have been gambled away on. Let's take all of the stock market executives' multimillion-dollar pay bonuses (they'll have to get by on their multimillion-dollar salaries alone) and give them to homeless veterans and unemployed workers with families, just to piss off those Wall Street guys. Let's open up the secret Presidential Archives that George locked down. Now that's some change I can believe in. Please, Barack, don't just give us the old, stale $1.99 McChange burger with hope sauce, freedom fries, and a war-sized Coke. And Joe Biden, stop talking about a "generated crisis" that will test our new president shortly after he takes office. You're just making everything too obvious.

Bush's Effect on Prayer

As his approval ratings steadily dropped since his high point on September 11, 2001, President Bush compelled Americans to look to a higher power.

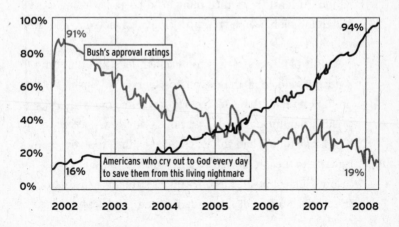

For the last eight years, our country under the leadership of George W. Bush has acted like a hormone-crazed teenaged boy on steroids. We've been stuck in a prolonged adolescence, caught in the confusing limbo between child and adult. Desperate to prove our manhood, we've bullied, name-called, and picked fights all over the globe. Still attached to childish fancies of acquiring ever more toys, we've maxed out our credit cards on ridiculously big trucks, homes, and TVs, never bothering to think about how we could actually pay for all of it. Being encouraged to "get out there and shop" by our enabler-in-chief didn't help. We haven't bothered to clean up after ourselves, trashing our rivers, skies, and forests and have removed oversight on consumer and worker protections. We need some parental-style oversight again, especially on the Lord of the Flies island that is Wall Street. We can't act like feral children anymore, just grabbing as much as we can without any consideration of the wider consequences of our actions. It's time to grow up, America. Don't be afraid. After making it through the Bush years, our eyes are opened to the chance at becoming a decent, thoughtful, fair, and sustainable nation. At least, it's a nice thought to keep you going as you search for a job, watch your 401(k) savings melt down, or lose your house.

But before we all get too excited, let's take the time to send out one final thank-you to George W. Bush. No one brought it realer than George. He gave us so many sharp, surprising, painful moments. Without George, we never would have known how bad things could get. Bush took our nation right up to the cliff's edge, to gaze down at the sharp rocks far below. He then pushed us off, sank us straight to the bottom of the ocean, dragged us into a thermal vent, and kept on digging.

Thankfully, his eight years are finally up, just before we hit the white-hot molten core of our economy. So thanks, George, from all of us who have managed to survive this long. This is our way of saying good-bye to you. We just look back, shake our heads in amazement, and then try to keep putting one foot in front of the other. We'll probably even let you retire peacefully, you slippery old Crawford crawdaddy. We won't follow up on that suggestion your dad made. We'll just party in the streets when you're gone, reminisce about all the wonderful times we've had, and vow to never let them happen again. Of course, if you end up in Slobodan Milosevic's old cell at the International Criminal Court, that would be fine with us too.

Vaya con dios, Señor Boosh! See you in hell.

Acknowledgments

Special thanks to Todd Brunner, Nick Gallo, Daniel Greenberg, Brandon Haynes, Chad Nackers, Randy Ostrow, Chris Pauls, Dan Rembert, Josh Saunders, and Brett Valley.

About the Author

MIKE LOEW was the graphics editor and a writer for *The Onion* from 1993 to 2007. He managed the graphics and contributed writing to *The Onion's* two bestsellers *Our Dumb Century* and *Our Dumb World*. He still contributes to *The Onion* and is the author of two previous books, *Tough Call* and *Citizen You!* (with Joe Garden and Randy Ostrow). He lives in Brooklyn, New York.